FOUR WHEEL DRIVING

Four Wheel Driving

Simon Newitt

OSPREY AUTOMOTIVE

Pages 2 and 3
For really serious mud-plugging, these bolt-on Bog Cogs make a dramatic difference to traction.
(Photo: Wessex UK plc).

PUBLISHER'S NOTE
Off-road driving is a potentially dangerous activity and should only be undertaken following the strictest safety precautions. The Publishers accept no responsibility for any loss or injury arising from any activities described in this book.

Published in 1991 by Osprey Publishing Ltd
59 Grosvenor Street, London W1X 9DA

© Simon Newitt 1991

All rights reserved. Apart from any fair dealing for the purpose of private study, research, criticism or review, as permitted under the Copyright, Designs and Patents Act, 1988, no part of this publication may be reproduced, stored in a retrieval system, or transmitted in any form or by any means, electronic, electrical, chemical, mechanical, optical, photocopying, recording, or otherwise, without prior written permission. All enquiries should be addressed to the Publishers.

British Library Cataloguing in Publication data

Newitt, Simon
Four wheel driving.
1 Cars
I. Title
629.222

ISBN 1-85532-144-0

Design Gwyn Lewis
Phototypeset by Keyspools, Golborne, Lancs
Printed in Great Britain by
BAS Printers Limited, Over Wallop, Hampshire

Contents

Foreword 7

Introduction 9

1 An introduction to 4WD vehicles 11

2 Buying a used 4WD vehicle 18

3 Learning to live with a 4WD 26

4 Off-road driving 32

5 Off-road competitions 44

6 Preparing for competition 54

7 The rubber solution 60

8 When you get stuck 70

9 Every winch way 74

10 Accessories for 4WD 86

11 Four-wheel drive expeditions 96

12 Camel Trophy – the last great adventure 102

13 The Ultimate Dirty Weekend? 112

The Off-Roader's Directory 118

About the Author

Simon Newitt was born in Singapore in March 1963, and lived for some time in the Far East before returning to England and a college education. He then spent several years studying business administration and management, before starting his own company in the 1980s.

He was introduced to off-road driving during an exhilarating ride in a friend's vehicle, and is now an accomplished driver in his own right and a great fan of the Range Rover. Like so many other people, Simon had to acquire all his driving skills by trial and error, working hard to bring himself up to a high standard by constant practice – despite dropping a brand new Range Rover on its side very early in his career. His consuming interest in driving techniques led him to a professional involvement in the design and marketing of several specialist off-road vehicles, and also resulted in an invitation to join the 1990 Camel Trophy expedition – an opportunity that he reluctantly had to turn down because of business commitments.

His ultimate ambitions are to open an off-road driving school and to organize safari-style holidays in Africa – catering especially for those who want plenty of expedition-standard driving, and an adventure holiday with real potential.

Acknowledgments

First, my grateful thanks go to Fiona ('Fizz') Carter, who, apart from taking many of the photographs, also gave me the encouragement and support I needed to actually complete the book. My thanks also go to Land Rover Ltd, for their very generous loan of the Range Rover Vogue Turbo Diesel, which I was most reluctant to hand back! To Land Rover Parts and Equipment Ltd for kindly providing the photographs of Discovery and Land Rover accessories. To H. Torosyan and Bearmach (London) Ltd, for allowing me to reproduce the article about vehicle accessories, and for the associated photographs. And to Chris Bennett Author of Osprey's forthcoming *Land Rover*.

My thanks also go to Nigel Quilter of Jardine P. R. and David Arthur of R. J. Reynolds for their help during the preparation of the Camel Trophy chapter, and for inviting me to the selection weekend. To Jim Bradley for his incomparable scribblings on buying and maintaining 4WD vehicles, and for his contribution to the vehicle recovery chapter. And to Ken and Julie Slavin of K & J Slavin (Quest) Ltd for the chapter on expedition preparation and driving.

My thanks go to Ronnie Dale for kindly agreeing to write the foreword, and to John and Diana Carter for letting me use the High Hurlands Estate and their Land Rover collection for much of the static photography.

Above all I am very grateful To John Beese and *Off-road and 4 Wheel Drive* magazine for providing photographs and allowing me to reproduce the sections on tyres and winching, and for the considerable help given during the preparation of the Off-road Directory section at the back of this book.

Happy off-roading.

Foreword

By Ronnie Dale – twice a Camel Trophy finalist and owner of one of Britain's leading off-road driver training schools.

In the beginning there were only three kinds of off-road driver – the explorer, the serviceman and the farmer – and none of them really seemed to appreciate how much fun they were having. The true explorers were all tucked away in the darkest parts of Africa or South America, and were far too busy with their own problems and discoveries to worry about the joys of off-road driving. The serviceman was a professional driver through and through, probably fed up with being told what to do all the time, and dismally unaware of the funny side of life – especially when he was churning up the training ground mud for the umpteenth time while his mates were downtown enjoying altogether more earthy pleasures. Farmers, as we all know, are far too busy to have any fun at all. The true nature of off-road driving, the sheer fun and excitement that can be had without too much expense, was almost entirely lost on these folk and therefore ignored until fairly recently.

Few people outside these 'privileged' groups drove early four-wheel drive (4WD) vehicles unless they absolutely had to. The vehicles themselves were all far too expensive, ridiculously noisy and unbearably spartan in their creature comforts. Over the last few years things have changed a lot. Motor manufacturers have now realized that the off-road image has a real profit potential, and their latest developments have made comfortable, dual-purpose vehicles available to a much wider audience. The secret is out at last, and four-wheel drive has become a highly prized part of the normal motoring scene.

With free access to plenty of rough farmland, I was able to start my off-road driving career quite early. That great feeling of satisfaction after getting the vehicle to places it had never been before was second only to the surprise on the faces of my uninitiated companions. The very idea of driving off into unknown territory has drained the colour from many a strong man, but with modern equipment and adequate knowledge these excursions can actually be accomplished with considerable confidence. One word of warning though, based on experience: always make sure that you *can* do what you set out to do – particularly before you show off your 'skills' to others. The number-one rule of all off-roaders should be *never show off and fail!*

Off-road driving is essentially no different from driving on normal roads. You will still need the same level of anticipation, skill, vehicle sympathy and above all safety, but in return you will have the extra spice, the ability to get away from others and appreciate the wilder parts of the world. A few years ago the off-road driver had to learn all his technique by trial and error, and experience was rarely passed on. Books like Simon's are now spreading the word that safe off-roading is not only great fun, but also far more accessible than it ever has been before. It demands as much skill from the driver as any other form of motor sport, but it can also be enjoyed by the rest of the family at the same time. In this it may be unique.

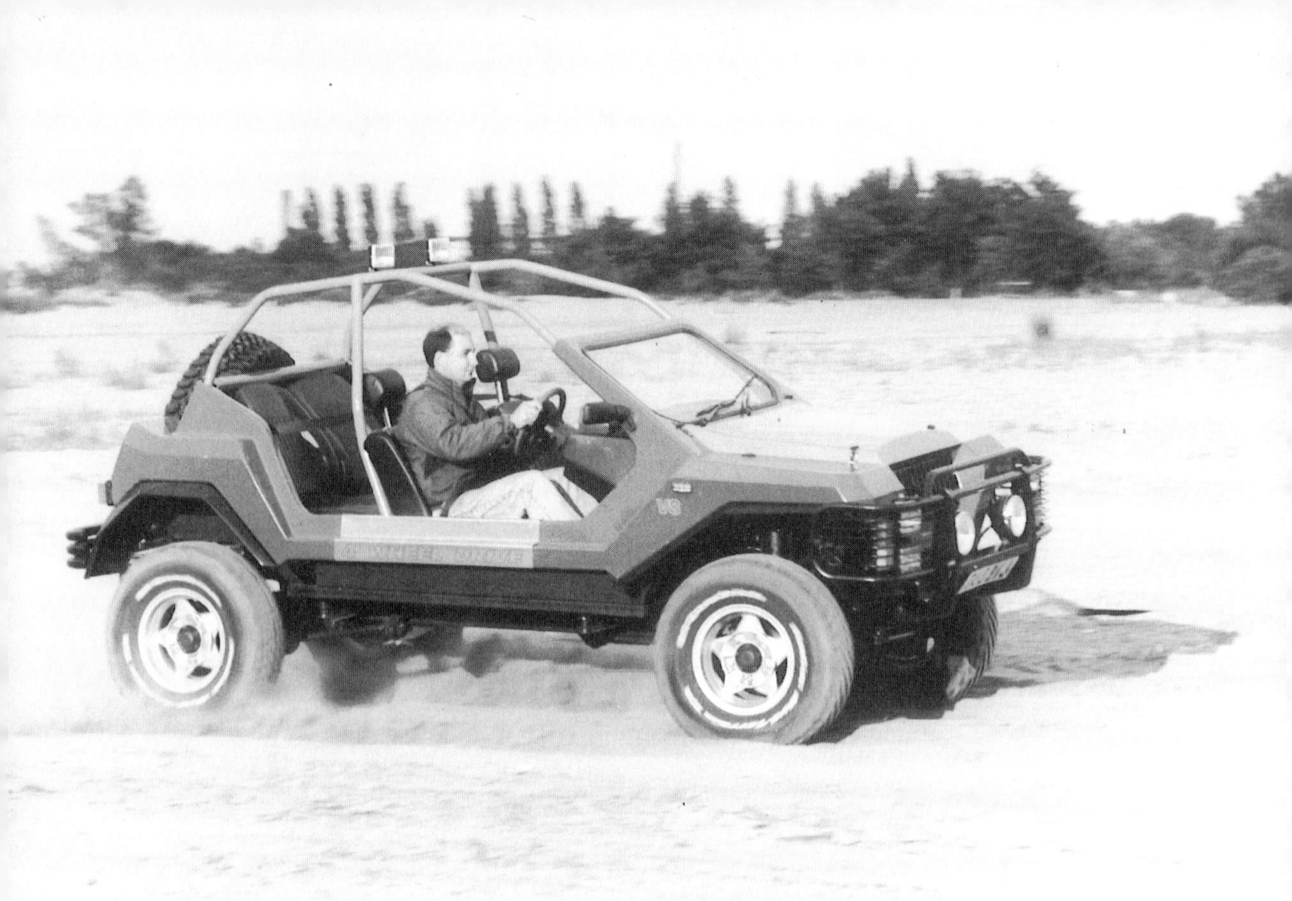

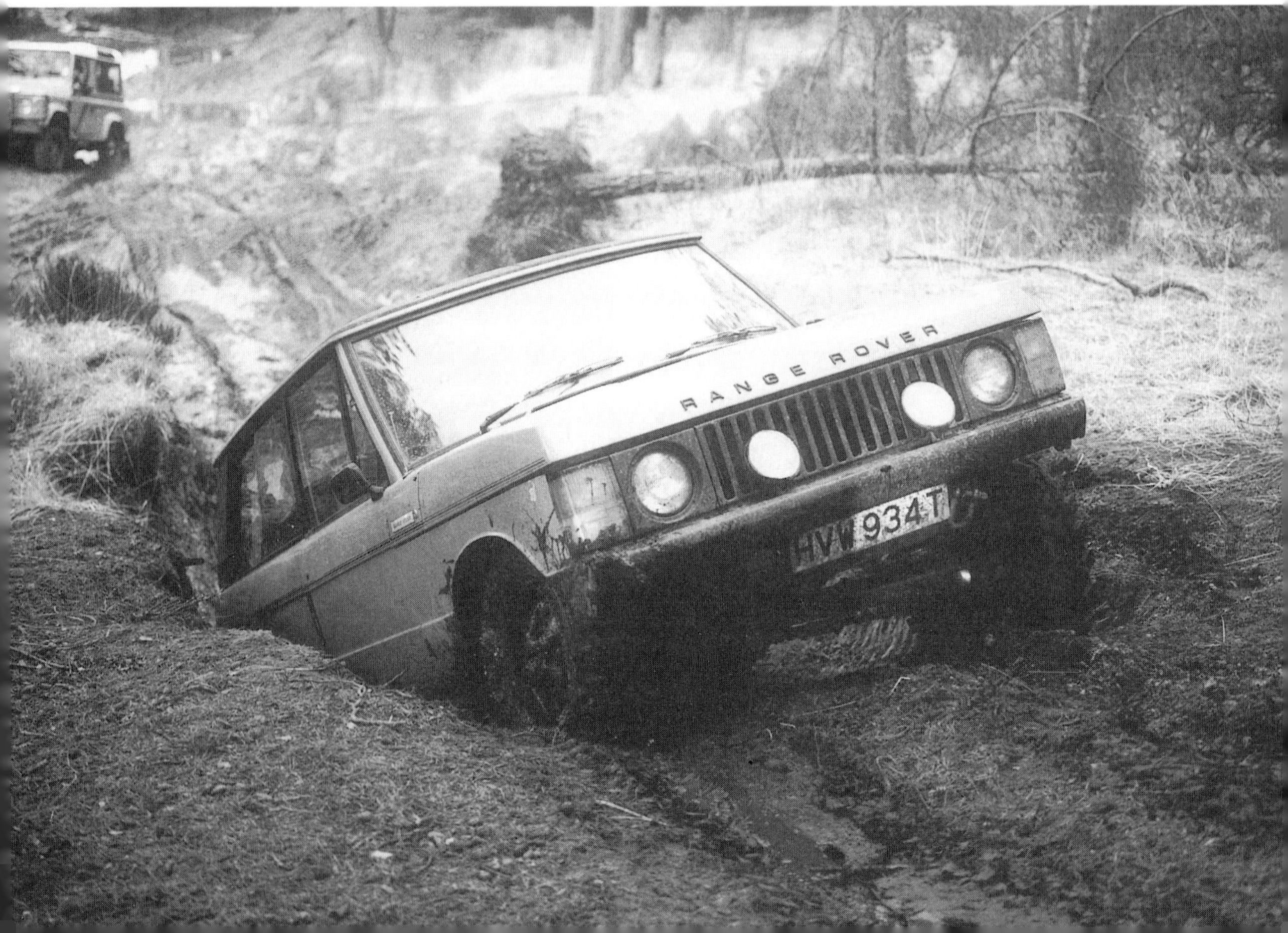
RANGE ROVER
HVW 934T

Introduction

Why is it that grown men and women are willing to spend vast sums of money on a beautifully prepared vehicle, and then drive it straight from the showroom into a local mud bath? This bizarre pattern of behaviour, which might well have originated in the twisted mind of a brilliant hosepipe salesman, is now considered entirely normal by the growing band of enthusiasts who devote much time and energy to a new hobby called off-road driving.

The past few years have seen a remarkable expansion in the availability of four-wheel drive vehicles. Most of these were probably acquired in the first place by safety conscious motorists for normal road use, but along with the growth in ownership has come an increasing awareness of the capabilities of 4WD in off-road conditions. Many clubs and societies have now been formed to promote and encourage the use of these vehicles, and judging by the number of drivers involved in off-road meetings, the future of the hobby – or sport if you prefer – is completely secure.

What is it about off-roading that makes it so enjoyable? In my case it provides an opportunity to get away from busy towns and overcrowded roads and return to nature; a chance to spend a day in the countryside far from the usual pressures of life, just relaxing with good company and a capable vehicle. Most clubs of course have a large social element, and delightful picnics, nature trails or group excursions can usually be arranged at the drop of a hat – but the competitive instinct among club drivers is never too far away. Many people regularly choose to pit their wits against each other by taking part in well-organized trials or competitive safaris, while others simply prefer to watch the events, or perhaps offer a helping hand by becoming a marshal or scorer for the day. Whatever aspect of off-roading eventually appeals to you, the hobby as a whole can offer considerable challenges, as well as a great deal of fun and enjoyment.

The aim of this book is to show new 4WD owners, or even those with some experience of the vehicles on normal roads, just how simple and safe off-road driving can be, and how you can get more involved in the social and competitive aspects of a splendid sporting hobby. The chapters will take you from a basic understanding of how the 4WD system works, through to buying and maintaining a vehicle, and on to a discussion of safe driving techniques for off-road conditions. There are also chapters about the basics of competitive driving, and a few ideas for those of you who are more adventurously inclined. There is also a reference section to help you make the most of your particular interest or vehicle. I hope the book will prove to be both useful and enjoyable, and that it will act as a ready source of information while you gain confidence and interest.

ABOVE LEFT
Stripped for action: this was a Range Rover!

LEFT
The original – and many would say, still the best, after more than two decades – being put through its paces. Try doing this in the family saloon ...

1
An introduction to 4WD vehicles

Off-road drivers tend not to take life too seriously, but a basic understanding of the principles of four-wheel drive is obviously important if you want to use a vehicle away from the highway while retaining most of its theoretical performance. In this section I will attempt to explain in simple terms how a 4WD system works, and interpret some of the more baffling terminology. This should enable you to stun the uninitiated with your obvious knowledge, and at least hold your own in a conversation with fellow conspirators.

Don't be unduly worried if you are still mystified at the end of the chapter, because you can always read it through again. Off-road vehicles are slightly more complicated than conventional cars, but they are really quite simple beasts when you understand which bit goes where, and why. The more familiar you are with the individual components, the simpler the whole drive system will seem.

Drive configurations

Off-road vehicles are basically divided into two camps, those with permanent four-wheel drive and those with a part-time 4WD system. The permanent arrangement ensures that all four road wheels are driven all the time. This has distinct advantages in many respects because it gives the vehicle limpet-like roadholding and startling performance from rest in the wet. Unfortunately the downside of having all four wheels permanently driven is a higher fuel consumption and increased tyre wear.

With a part-time system only two wheels (generally the rears) are driven permanently. When the vehicle encounters a loose surface the driver manually engages the forward transmission to complete the 4WD system, and then disengages as soon as he returns to a tarmac road. These systems give superb off-road performance, but should never be left engaged during normal on-road driving. If this vital rule is ignored, chronic transmission problems are bound to occur.

Petrol or Diesel?

With today's technology, diesels can provide an overall performance that is pretty close to (though different from) a modern petrol engine. Both engines have significant advantages and disadvantages to the off-road driver, and any decision between the two should be based on sensible economic or usage factors. I would be the first to admit that nothing can beat the sound of a lovely light-alloy V8 working hard on a steep slope, or the smell of a big petrol engine ticking over after a play in the mud, but despite these very personal reactions to petrol units, I still prefer a diesel for my own use.

Apart from its general smoothness, the petrol engine does have one big advantage over most diesels. As soon as you touch the loud pedal on a petrol engine the power comes straight in, allowing you to ascend steep slopes at low revs by feeding in just enough drive to keep the vehicle moving, but without having to use so much that grip is broken. The petrol engine also has enough acceleration and power to keep you up with the pack on motorways and freeways.

Unfortunately, the penalty for all this performance has got to be high fuel consumption: moving a vehicle weighing perhaps two tons, with the drag factor of a battered house-brick and a transmission

Mercedes-Benz 300GD short-wheel-base takes to the water.

system as complex as that on a railway locomotive, is not going to do your bank balance any good at all. Most man-sized petrol-engined 4WD vehicles have a consumption figure of around 20 mpg, and unless you own the bank (or know a man who does) it might be advisable to consider the diesel alternative.

Far and away my personal favourite, a diesel engine offers several benefits to the off-road driver which more than compensate for its one acknowledged weakness. Modern diesels bear no comparison to the clattery, oil-spewing monsters of yesteryear, and thanks to turbocharging they are often just as fast as their petrol counterparts; they are also much quieter now, and use only half the fuel of an equivalent petrol engine. Perhaps the biggest single advantage of the diesel system is its complete lack of exposed electrics. The absence of ignition-related wiring (distributor, HT leads, etc) gives you far more freedom off-road, because nothing can get seriously wet when the vehicle ploughs into deep water. A petrol engine can drown remarkably easily, no matter how well-protected you may think it is.

Because of its requirement for compressive ignition, the diesel engine also operates at a much higher compression ratio than any conventional petrol engine. This ratio is generally around the 22:1 mark (compared with 8 or 9:1 for petrol), which immediately gives you a phenomenal braking effect. Coming off the accelerator in a diesel vehicle is like driving into a brick wall, and the control that this gives you on a severe downslope is truly amazing.

The main disadvantage of a diesel vehicle is really an off-road problem and is unlikely to degrade its road performance. The turbo normally starts to operate at a specific engine speed (usually 2000/2500 rpm), and without its influence there is precious little power available to move the vehicle. This means you will need to accelerate fast enough to cut the turbo in, and thereafter keep the revs reasonably high to maintain the extra power. With a petrol engine you could trickle up a slope in third gear, but with a diesel you would probably have to charge up in second, using revs and the turbo to make up the difference in performance. With this technique the wheels are sometimes scrabbling for grip near the top, and you could be left frantically trying to remember how to handle an aborted ascent! Although this kind of thing can be a problem with diesels, they more than make up for it with their remarkable fuel economy and bottom-end torque. For high mileage drivers – especially those where a 4WD is the main vehicle – they come highly recommended.

Transmission systems

The transmission systems of off-road 4WD vehicles are rather more complicated than those on a conventional two-wheel drive car because they have two separate gear trains – a low range for cross-country driving and a high range for normal road use. Manual and automatic gearboxes are both obtainable, but for serious off-road use – particularly with petrol driven vehicles – a manual box is generally preferred because it gives better engine braking. With a manual box in first gear of its low range, you can gently ease the vehicle down a steep slope at less than walking pace. With an automatic box, descending a slope under engine braking can be an interesting challenge. The low range first gear in an automatic box is roughly equivalent to second in a low range manual, and this inevitably brings you down more quickly. If the gearbox is attached to the low compression-ratio of a petrol engine (rather than a high braking-efficiency diesel), you can often arrive at the bottom somewhat faster than you intended. This is an important point to remember when choosing a gearbox, because hitting the brakes on a loose or slippery surface is not a good idea if you want to arrive at the bottom with your dignity and you vehicle intact.

Although you miss out on the very lowest gear, automatic boxes do have distinct advantages in the right vehicle. If you are careless enough to get stuck half way up a steep slope for instance, you can forget all the fancy footwork needed with a manual gearbox; simply keep your toe on the brake pedal while you slide the auto selector into reverse, and away you go. You will not stall an automatic on an aborted ascent. Also, if you have a predilection for swimming with your 4WD and you hit something immovable in the water, at least the engine will keep going. A manual box under these circumstances will almost certainly stall, filling your exhaust pipe with water and wrecking any chance of a restart.

The best combination I ever drove was a meaty 3.5 litre turbocharged diesel with an automatic

AN INTRODUCTION TO 4WD VEHICLES

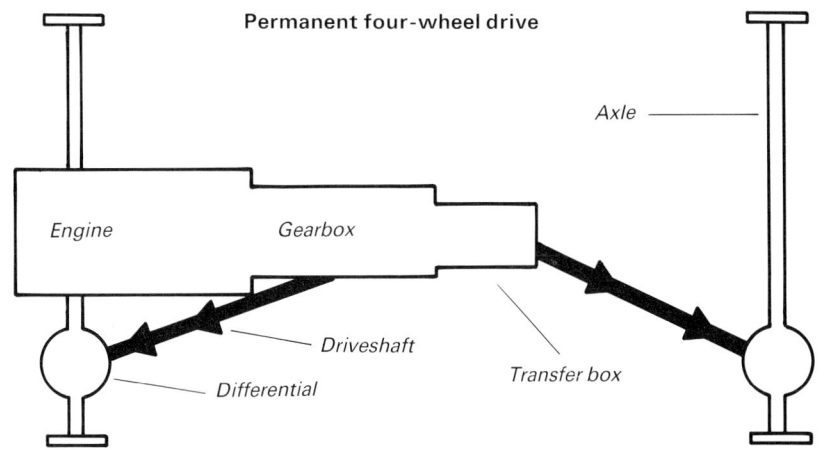

On a permanent four-wheel drive system the front and rear driveshafts are both under power at all times, but they are not linked together until the central differential lock (housed in the transfer box) is engaged.

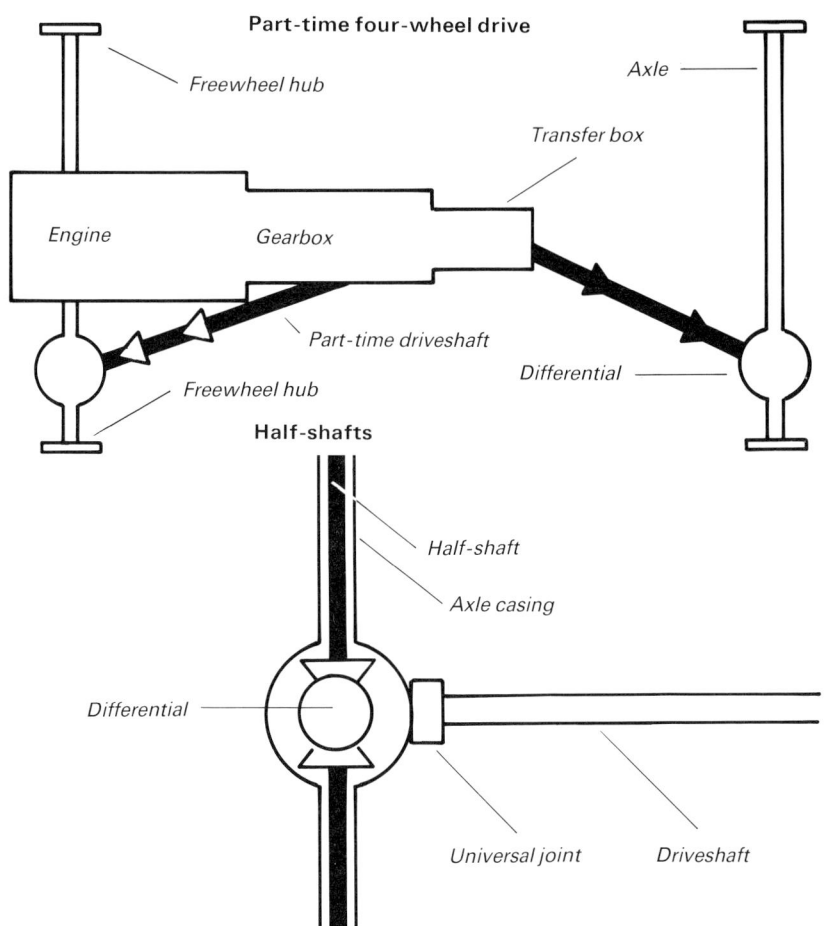

With a part-time 4WD system the front driveshaft is only under power when needed. The freewheel hubs prevent its unnecessary rotation when the vehicle is being used in two-wheel drive.

The two half-shafts are independent of each other, but are dynamically linked by the differential.

FOUR WHEEL DRIVING

Land Rover Discovery 200 TDi; Land Rover offered turbo diesel in response to the success the Germans and Japanese had enjoyed with the powerplant, Nobody could accuse them of rushing into things: TD had been on the market for a decade and more before they released their own version.

gearbox. The high compression braking effect of the engine easily made up for any shortcomings in the auto box, and steep ascents or descents were an absolute doddle. If they are well matched, the auto/diesel combination is probably the most versatile for general work. Petrol engines with automatic gearboxes should be avoided like the plague, especially for arduous off-road conditions.

The transfer box

The transfer box on a 4WD is a multi-function second gearbox, which is always immediately aft of the main unit. As its name implies, its primary function is to transfer the drive from the engine through two shafts to the front and rear axles. On a vehicle with permanent 4WD the transfer box also houses the differential lock (of which more later), and on a part-time 4WD system the box incorporates the locking mechanism for the front drive train. On both permanent and part-time systems, the transfer box also houses the reduction gear to allow selection of the high and low range gear ratios. The high range gearing is really no different from the gearbox on a conventional car, and the ratios confer normal road performance. The low range on the other hand is a bit special, and is normally used for off-road driving, or for any other situation where precise control is needed. Both ranges use the same actual gears in the main box, but low range is accessed by introducing a reduction gear between the output shaft of the transfer box and the drive shafts.

The shafts

If you enter the world of serious off-road driving you may occasionally hear your new found partners in muddy crime muttering darkly about drive shafts or half-shafts. These are basically the rods of metal that direct the drive from the transfer box into each axle, and then out to the wheels. The primary drive shafts run from the transfer box itself down to the front and rear axles, and because the axles are sprung, each attachment point has to be achieved through a universal joint. The need to vary the effective length of a drive shaft (also due to the springing), is normally accommodated by a splined sliding joint at one end of each shaft.

The half-shafts are found inside each axle, and run from either side of the differential out to the wheels: no universal joints are necessary in this case because the axle itself is one rigid assembly. If any final drive system can be said to have a weak spot, then half-shafts must surely be up among the prizes! As you become more adventurous with your vehicle, you may well have the misfortune to 'blow' a half-shaft one day. This happens when too much power is fed through the axle, and the shaft simply decides that it can't take any more abuse, and snaps. Half-shafts are generally longer on one side of the axle than on the other, and because of the lever-moment involved, the long side always seems to break first. The frustrating thing is that replacements are only available in pairs, so lots of drivers end up with a fair old collection of short but redundant pieces of expensive metal.

Differential locks

All vehicles fitted with permanent 4WD feature a central differential in the transfer box. This separates the front and rear drive trains into two systems, and allows each to spin independently on hard surfaces. Without this separation, all minor differences in the distance each wheel travels round a corner, or even variations in wheel diameter due to tyre wear or pressure, will rapidly accumulate and 'wind up' the transmission, leading ultimately to complete seizure. Loose surfaces generally allow these differences to 'unwind' naturally and progressively, and this permits the two drive trains to be locked together to increase traction. The locking mechanism for this system is called a central differential lock.

All 4WD vehicles can be fitted with cross-axle differential locks. These replace a normal differential inside the axle casing, and in theory can be fitted to both front and rear axles. A self-locking (or limited slip) differential usually operates independently of any driver control by sensing the amount of traction being fed through to each wheel. If one wheel starts to spin, the unit operates, and drive is automatically fed through to the wheel that has stopped, giving it the traction necessary to maintain progress. The only disadvantage of this system is the need for a degree of torque on the stopped wheel in order to lock the differential. If you have a wheel waving in the air (not uncommon on really rough terrain), there is no torque and the system fails to operate: applying the brakes slightly can often restore the situation, allowing you to continue without losing too much pride.

A fully locking differential performs the same function as the self-locking variety, but it has to be operated by the driver from a control in the cab. Fully locking diffs are a wonderful aid to off-road traction, but please be wary of fitting them to the front axle, because they severely limit the difference between the rotational speeds of the two front wheels. This is fine for blasting up a steep slope in a vaguely straight line, but if you try to take any kind of bend the steering will stubbornly refuse to co-operate because the inner wheel cannot slow down to allow the outer to run round it. Unless you spend 95 per cent of your time in really severe off-road conditions you will only need a diff lock on the rear axle: a lock at both ends is complete overkill.

FOUR WHEEL DRIVING

Evidence of the relative buoyancy of the 'recreational vehicle' market: Vauxhall enters the fray for the first time in 1991 with the Frontera. The LWB version offers the choice of 2.4-Litre petrol or 2.3-Litre turbo diesel engines.

Freewheel hubs

Freewheel hubs are fitted to the front axles of part-time 4WD vehicles to improve their fuel economy during normal road driving. Without them the entire front drive train (half-shafts, differential and drive shafts) will spin with the wheels, adding unnecessary resistance to what should be a fairly light rolling motion. This resistance mops up energy from the engine, and increases wear on the front tyres and drive components. Fitting freewheel hubs allows you to disconnect all the heavy driving machinery from the front wheels when the vehicle is being used in two-wheel drive, theoretically saving fuel and increasing component life.

The hubs are available in automatic or manual form. The automatic variety will engage as soon as you select four-wheel drive, ensuring a fully secured drive train in either gear range. Back on a tarmac surface they will automatically disengage when you select two-wheel drive, usually by reversing for a few feet. Manual hubs are potentially a lot more exciting because they need positive action from the driver. Selecting four-wheel drive without getting out of the cab to engage each hub in turn, effectively gives you a cleverly disguised two-wheel drive vehicle! All the gear levers are in the right place, and the machinery is whizzing around happily, but if the front wheels are not connectd you might as well give up. Please remember to engage these hubs *before* you start playing in the mud! I found out about this the hard way while testing a new vehicle with part-time 4WD; after getting horribly stuck it quickly dawned on me that it was generally easier to engage the hubs while you could actually see them, rather than grope around in 2 ft of glutinous Hampshire mud trying to do it all by feel. You have been warned.

The vital angles

All over the world you will find men hunched over pots of ale, earnestly discussing approach and departure angles and the meaning of life in relation to off-roading. The angles are especially important to competitive drivers because they determine the obstacle clearances at each end of a vehicle. In basic form the approach angle is measured by taking a line from a point on the bumper, and running it down to the ground so that it just touches the forward face of the tyre tread. The angle between that line and flat ground tells you the maximum gradient of an uphill slope that can be approached without demolishing the front end of your vehicle. The majority of 4WDs have an approach angle of 35–40 degrees, which is generally considered acceptable for off-road. Beware though, of the demented vehicle stylist who hangs a fancy bit of plastic or a couple of lights below the bumper: anything fixed in that area will drastically reduce your approach angle, and is a dead cert for demolition as soon as you start making mud pies.

The departure angle is measured in the same way, but it refers to the other end of the vehicle. Be careful not to spoil a good departure angle with rear fog lamps or a towing hook: the lamps can be wiped off without you even noticing, but substantial bits of ironmongery such as a towbar can cause the backend to dig into the ground and result in the vehicle getting well and truly hung up. This kind of carelessness leads to a complete loss of forward momentum, and often results in a colourful volley of Anglo-Saxon language from the driver. As with the front of the vehicle, anything that can be removed from below the bumper should be removed before going off-road!

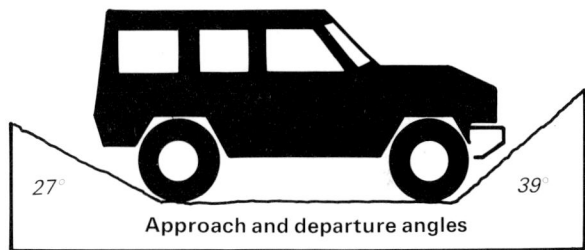

Approach and departure angles

The approach and departure angles are important because they determine the front and rear end obstacle clearance of the vehicle.

2
Buying a used 4WD vehicle

This chapter is slightly adapted from an article that originally appeared in Overlander 4 × 4 *magazine, and appears by kind permission of its author, Jim Bradley*

It is true to say that there is a lot more to an off-road vehicle than there is to a normal 'box-on-wheels' saloon car. Nevertheless, if approached in a sensible and cautious manner, it is still possible for a person of ordinary experience to select a good secondhand 4WD without being had.

I will set out in as simple a way as practicable, a general guide for those trying to buy a Land Rover for the first time. In choosing a Land Rover as my subject vehicle I am not denigrating in any way the other makes of off-road motor car. It is just that there are a lot more Land Rovers on the secondhand market, thus giving a wider choice. They also last a lot longer than the rest, spares are available for about 100 per cent of all models, and lastly – and to my mind most important – they are British.

The best way to approach the whole subject is to set matters out under individual headings for each aspect. This makes it a lot easier for me, and gives an outline order in which matters should proceed.

Fuel

The choice between petrol and diesel (and to a smaller extent, LPG) could be a chapter in itself. However, we will stick to a general comparison between the two major fuels.

Petrol engines undoubtedly use more fuel, and they need careful and frequent tuning to avoid low power and consumption horrors. They start more easily than diesels and, weight for weight, give a lot more power. Petrol engined vehicles make up the bulk of 4WDs.

Diesel vehicles are generally more sluggish (Merc 'G' Wagons excepted); the engines go on for ages without too much attention, but with the penalty of astronomic bills for any major repair. They can be a pig to start, especially in cold weather, and can be subject to fuel freezing. They vibrate a lot and are often very noisy. A run in a Land Rover with a Perkins conversion was once described to me as a voyage beyond the threshold of real pain. A diesel has lots of low down torque which is a useful advantage on the rough, while the petrol model will rev a lot higher and keep you in the overtaking league on the open road.

One final factor in this brief look at the subject. Those of us who depend on a 4WD to get to work or other vital functions, sometimes worry about fuel availability. You must take into account that it is legal to store as much diesel as you wish on your own domain. To store petrol you have to acquire a licence and satisfy all sorts of requirements, which makes the job hideously expensive. For diesel all you need is a sound secondhand heating-oil tank, a stand, and a delivery pipe that will reach the vehicle's fuel hole. Oh yes, and a ruddy great lock.

Short or long?

For most ordinary mortals Land Rovers come in two lengths (I crave the indulgence of specialist factions of the Land Rover world, but I am trying to keep it simple). A long wheel base (LWB) Land Rover has lots of space, is a bit higher, and usually performs slightly less well than the short wheel base (SWB) model because it is heavier. For the same reason the longer vehicle can be a handful and a half on cross-country trips, especially on any kind of sharp hill crest. The secondhand LWB Land Rover is invariably an ex-fleet vehicle (all the usual public utility outfits) and will frequently be of high mileage, but it may have been regularly serviced on a scheduled basis. The SWB models are often ex-agriculture, which can mean very sketchy servicing and a history of towing great trailer loads of livestock all over the place.

In summary, the first-time buyer would be well advised to think in terms of a short model unless he needs the capacity of the long job.

A final word – all Land Rovers are a touch higher than most cars. This leads to problems when trying to fit them in the garage. They live outside as readily as a cow, but due to the extra height they can be as awkward as a cow to get into a garage. A lovely tale was mentioned in local circles some time ago, about a proud owner who bought one of those full-length roof racks for his LWB, and then fitted it in the comfort of his garage. Happy with his efforts, he decided to do the natural thing and have a cruise around the neighbourhood for all to admire this galvanized monster on the roof. With all his usual confidence he reversed out of the garage, only to be engulfed in falling masonry as the roof rack made room for itself with very expensive results.

There are lots of beautiful old Land Rovers around, but choose carefully and buy from a real enthusiast if possible.

Where to look

Some garages have the odd Land Rover among their secondhand cars. These will usually be in fair condition, having been put through the workshop ... maybe. Please bear in mind that a common practice is for salesmen to have the commission on a new car sale withheld until the trade-in has been sold. This means most will be keen to haggle, but will also wait until you are just about hooked before deftly sliding in the magic VAT figure. Now I'm as honest as I have to be, but I detest having to donate a large number of my precious beer vouchers to the Government so that they can waste them. Auctions can be a big lure, although again VAT can be applicable. Auctions also mean that the time and facilities for examination are limited, and a few nasty people use them to dispose of Land Rovers in poor condition.

The columns of *Exchange and Mart*, 4 × 4 magazines and local papers will usually provide a suitable number of candidates. Lastly, word of mouth. Mentioning your desire to own a Land Rover to the barman at your local, or to your social worker etc, often produces results.

I don't recommend advertising for a Land Rover unless you have seen a good one being driven by a bloke who you know is either leaving the country soon, has just been breathalysed or just looks silly.

Otherwise every sharp guy and his brother will arrive at your door in the middle of tea-time wanting a huge sum for a pile of junk, and oh boy, are some of these people hard to get rid of! Advertising is usually unproductive.

Confrontation

So, you have had a phone conversation with a bloke who wants to sell a Land Rover. You have asked him to hose off the underneath and have it standing on a dry, hard surface if possible. Take a friend with you, ideally one who knows all the little ways of Land Rovers. Get someone to show you in advance what all the levers do and which door to enter by. Don't show up in your best clothes, wear a boiler-suit with a ruler pocket in which you have secreted a stout screwdriver. Your buddy, regardless of what he does or does not know about the subject in hand, must agree with everything you say, and vice versa.

Turn up on time and have a suitable quantity of dog biscuits in your pocket (Land Rover owners often have teeth-infested hounds which can be a wee bit protective towards the master's transport). Sweets for the kids can be a bonus too, if only to get a cup of tea and a chance to wash your hands at the termination of proceedings.

Always, always go in daylight, with enough of the stuff in hand to get the job done, but also take a torch to have a peer into the mucky corners.

Examination

Assuming that the object of your attention is there before you in reasonable light, walk all the way round it slowly. Then do it again a little further away. The vehicle should stand four-square on the ground and not sag in any direction. Look along the body sides and then, with the wheels dead ahead, look along them at hub height. You may find that there is a 'crab' effect, which means either body or chassis distortion. In good light, the vehicle should be all one shade of each colour. Now, it is not too big a sin if one wing is a slightly different shade, but if everything from the doors forward is different, it might just mean that there has been a major repair at some time. Doors should be a reasonable fit in all cases, and should close without a big slam. More about the body-beautiful later.

Engine The heart of any vehicle is the power unit, and the Land Rover is no exception. Most of them will be filthy, unless the vendor has steam cleaned the engine bay, in which case it will be difficult to see if there are any oil leaks. Check for broken engine-mounting rubbers, loose dynamo or alternator, oil weeps at the head gasket seam (the one where the cylinder head goes on to the engine block), and then invite our man to start up. You will have put your hand on the top of the radiator already, to check if he has had a warm-up first to disguise a bad starter. The engine, if petrol, should fire from cold almost at once, with the starter spinning things over at a good lick. A diesel will require about 30 sec pre-heat, then spin over slower than a petrol engine before firing up with a moderate cloud of white smoke from the exhaust. This smoke should disappear after a few blips of the throttle, and a fast tick-over on the hand throttle should be even with no 'gusting' or 'hunting'. Get the engine hot enough for the thermostat to open, which is indicated by the top hose going from cold to warm. Take off the oil filler cap and watch for 'chuffing' and/or oil fumes. A moderate amount of both is acceptable but too much indicates a worn unit. I cannot go into the full story of knocks and rumbles, but a rumble when the throttle is opened can be main bearings on their way out, while a harsh rattle on starting usually means that big-end bearings are shot. All bad news. Look for a drop of water from under the water pump. This gland is a sure-fire leaker if the vehicle has stood for any length of time, and is also sometimes visible as a rust line at six o'clock on the pump body.

With the engine stopped, get your mate to press down the clutch pedal, and then release it. Taking your screwdriver from its place of concealment, lever the crankshaft pulley back towards the engine. It might just visibly move. Then get matey to floor the clutch again. If that pulley moves forward more than is just visible, it is time you were on your way. End float on a crankshaft is bad news. Now have a look to see if any oil is leaking. A bit from the front pulley seal is not too bad, but any significant loss from the hole on the lower front of the clutch housing (right behind the engine) can be a big job to cure. Haul out the dipstick. New oil tells you little, other than the fact that it has been changed. If the oil is clear and new, look inside the oil filler cap and breather. Lots of white muck will tell you that you have a bit of a puffer on your hands. Grey oil is real trouble. This is caused by water, usually coolant, getting into the oil. Could be a head gasket blown, or more commonly in a diesel, a cracked head. Real trouble.

Both diesel and petrol engines should run sweetly and not peter out at any time. They are poor liars, and will soon tell you if all is not well.

Gearbox This needs a drive so we will kick for touch on this subject for now, other than to say that an underneath inspection should not show any large-scale leakage. The rubber mountings often go, but are simple to replace.

Chassis The chassis is the big black/brown thing that everything else is hung on. Major rust points, which you look for with your screwdriver while your mate gets the vendor to show him the toilet, are to be found on all outriggers (bits that stick out from the main fore and aft rails); the rear cross-member; and on the rear spring mounts of LWB models. On the underside of these parts there is a drain hole. If this has been bunged up, water will be trapped inside and tinworm will have struck. Poke your finger into the larger drain holes. Internal corrosion produces large scales of rust that lie in the bottom of the chassis. Look closely at the fuel tank bearers, bulkhead bearers, and all of the chassis from the rear wheel arches to the back cross-members. Give it a sharp rap with the screwdriver. Sound metal usually goes 'bong', while badly corroded metal goes 'thud' and frequently falls away to leave a big hole. Don't forget to feel the upper parts of all box sections because lots of people make a fair job of welding these, but only a real pro takes the body off and does the tops. Run your fingers (now bleeding freely from cuts inflicted by rusty metal) along the chassis near to where the springs are mounted. Any ripples in the flat surfaces might mean that the vehicle has had a major prang, and the chassis is buckled. Now check the cross-members under the clutch housing and gearbox. These are often caught on obstacles on rough ground and damaged. The gearbox cross-member may even be torn off in bad cases, while the beam under the clutch housing can be pushed up until it makes contact, which sends engine vibrations all through the vehicle.

Propshafts There are two of these, both more or less the same except for length. Grab hold of each end, and give them a good shake and twist. Any movement should be minimal and the ends should be firmly bolted to the differential or gearbox flanges. Each shaft has a sliding joint which allows it to vary in length as the axles rise and fall with suspension movement. Full marks if these each have a protective boot. There should be no free play, or severe vibration at speed will result. Remember this on your test run. While on the subject of drive, place the vehicle out of gear with the parking brake off, but with the wheels chocked in both directions: now grab hold of the prop shafts and turn them both ways to see how much backlash there is in the differentials. Any more than a quarter turn is bad.

Front axle At each end of the front axle are the swivels – the dread of all Land Rover mechanics. In most cases examination will show you a large, spherical device, which disappears into a housing, on to which the brake back plate is fitted. In all cases oil will be issuing from them in small amounts (which is quite normal), but not to such an extent that it is seen to drip. These balls are chromed, and pitting of the surface will soon destroy the oil seal and all the lovely lubricant comes charging out. A little pitting can be cured with some emery cloth and a new seal, but bad pitting or total rust will mean an expensive ball transplant in the near future. Some axles, particularly on ex-military models, are gaitered in this region. Old gaiters in good order are acceptable, but a set of nice new ones could mean that someone is trying to hide something. Jack up the front axle, and when you are sure the whole thing is safe, grasp the wheel at top and bottom and have a good shake. More than a little movement is trouble. If your mate puts his foot on the brake and the movement diminishes, the fault is in the wheel bearing: if not, it is the top swivel. If the movement is not too excessive, both can be corrected to some extent by adjustment. Look at the point where the brake drum goes over the backplate. Goo emitting from here means either a hub seal up the creek or a leaking brake cylinder. Not too bad to fix, but bear it in mind for the road test because a sudden application of brakes could treat you to a cathartic experience of drastic proportions.

Rear axle The rear axle is more or less the same as the front, except that there are no swivels to worry about, so we can progress to the . . .

FOUR WHEEL DRIVING

Suspension On the Land Rover there are leaf springs all round, shock absorbers of telescopic type, and large rubber bump stops.

All the springs must be checked for broken leaves, especially near the eyes at the end of the main leaf. These eyes have silentbloc rubber/metal bushes which are a press fit. If they are loose they wear the shackle bolt with expensive results. There are similar bushes in the chassis at the rear of the front spring, and on hangers at the back of the rear spring. Similar inspection please, but remember this: renewing the bush in the chassis at the front end is a nightmare of a job – like trying to poke butter into a hedgehogs nostrils with a red hot needle.

Look now at the spring hangers, the pairs of short arms which connect the rear of each spring to the chassis. The front ones should be almost vertical, while the rear ones should lay at an angle of no more than 45 degrees to the vertical. In all cases they should be more or less the same on each side. Rust will splay the leaves of an old worn spring, and is a prelude to fracture. Also, the ends of the shorter leaves have a nasty tendency to wear into the lower side of the longer leaf above. Again a sign of potential fracture.

Most Land Rover springs are either left-handed or right-handed, and they come in normal or heavy-duty. They also vary in the number of leaves, and to complicate matters even further, the front springs on a diesel vehicle are heavier than those on the petrol variety. Thus an oldish Land Rover could support an astonishing variety of springery, largely salvaged from wrecks.

Shock absorbers either work or they don't. You can't mend them, so those that have fluid issuing from the top shroud or are bent can be considered out of action. They have rubber bushes top and bottom, and the lower ones wear quickly and often have a lot of movement on the retaining pin. Sometimes the lower bushes are long gone. A bad sign. Rear axles have check straps which last about two years and drop off. They are seldom missed.

Brakes One of the better aspects of the Land Rover is its massive drum brakes. On all but the very latest SWB models the front and rear brakes are common. The LWB model has larger 11 in. brakes and usually a servo, which can be a big help but is also something else to go wrong.

Check all drums for leakage, and check the master cylinder by peering up into the hole from which the brake pedal appears. Then check all metal brake pipes carefully and suspect any which have recently been undersealed. A cover-up can be detected by looking at the gland nuts at the ends of the pipes. If they are claggy, then they have been there a long time and so has the pipe. Award maximum points for pipes which have been carefully replaced with stuff called Kunifer, which is far superior to the traditional steel. Make sure all pipes have been anchored where Rover originally intended. Runs of piping waving about is a recipe for trouble. The flexible hoses should be in good clean order, and free from cracks when pushed over to one side near to a union. The rear one is right in line for oil splash from a leaking differential pinion seal, which is a dead cert MOT failure and dangerous too.

The pedal should not have any side play, and you should meet firm resistance after no more than an inch of travel. Any pumping needed to produce a braking effect is suspect.

The hand brake is on the rear of the gearbox so there are no cable problems. Do not be too dismayed at a bit of oil dripping from the hand brake drum; this is common and a new seal and linings usually corrects matters. The lever ratchet often packs up and is similarly a simple job.

Do not try to test the hand brake on the move. You will probably tear it off the gearbox and the owner will be quite justified in assaulting you.

Wheels and tyres Check that all tyres are the same ply-type and size. A radial and cross-ply mix is dangerous, usually illegal and can lead to catastrophic transmission wind-up in four-wheel drive. The wheels should all be the same size, and this can be checked by comparing the numbers stamped on the wheel centres near the stud holes ($5.00F \times 16$ for SWB models and $5.5F \times 16$ for LWB). The LWB models have two different types of wheel offset. The later type with the wider part on the outside are best, and are the only sensible wheel rims to use if 205×16 radials are fitted.

Look for rim damage and obvious buckling of wheels, and don't forget the spare. Look for cuts, sidewall bulges and uneven wear on the tread surfaces. A tyre with lots of wear on the inside edge of the thread has probably been turned on the rim, so carefully check the inside sidewall. You might

22

BUYING A USED 4WD VEHICLE

The compact engine compartment of a Land Rover 90. Buying second-hand, there is no point in pretending to knowledge you don't have when it comes to the powerplant. If you can't take along a knowledgeable companion, follow the checks listed here – and listen as well as look. (Photo: Dennis Baldry).

just find a cut the size of a smile lurking there. I don't mind too much about tyres unless it seems obvious that the vendor has collected a 'selling set' from the discard piles at his local tyre company.

Steering Have a hauling and shoving session on all track-rod ends and drag-link joints. Check for oil leaks from the steering box and its slave relay on the front cross-member. If a relay dries out you might just be able to rescue it with oil, but then again you might not. Check that the steering box is well anchored to the front bulkhead and support plate, and that the relay is also secure.

Prod your friend awake and get him to move the steering wheel through an arc of about 40–60 degrees. Check each ball joint, and the drop arm from the steering box to the drag-link. That large nut can work loose, and if it does the drop arm will slop about on its splines. The relay shaft must have no sideways movement at all. Evict your long-suffering ally from the warmth of the cab and grab the steering wheel. Try to move it towards and away from you. There should be no movement.

Body Lift any mats in the driver and passenger footwells. You might then find yourself viewing the ground under the vehicle. Rust also strikes at the bottom of the door pillars, in the door tops and the frames of the door bottoms, and in the headlamp areas of the Series III models. A visual inspection of the alloy parts of the body should only reveal corrosion in the most abused of examples. Expect lots of dents and scrapes, but badly mended tears are unacceptable. Hardtops tend to leak around the seam joining the roof to the gutter, but this can be cured. Door seals are very pricey so if they are in good nick, so much the better. The same may be said for door catches and locks. I also like to see clean untorn seats, but this is not a big problem other than the cost if you want to replace them.

Electrics All the bits that are powered by electricity must work without having to be clouted or kicked into action. Try everything, and check that when all the electrics are on, the ammeter or voltmeter holds its own against the current drain. Straggling wires and obviously amateur cable installations are to be treated with great suspicion. The battery must have a dry external appearance, without large crystal growths on the connections. It should be a fairly large affair and be clamped into position, otherwise you will turn your engine bay into an electrolyte cocktail the first time you hit a decent bump.

Look carefully at the wiring to any trailer socket. This is the usual source of a short circuit because folk often do it themselves, and the connectors are commonly subjected to a battering of clag under the rear offside wing.

A word here about ex-military models with 24 volt systems. They are a curse and an abomination, and if you must buy one change it to 12 volts for the sake of your sanity.

Extra equipment Land Rovers can be fitted with all sorts of extra gear from spotlights to snowploughs (just look at all the glossy brochures). The usual style includes overdrive and free-wheel hubs, steering dampers and load assisters. These all have one thing in common – they either work or they do not. Simple isn't it?

Winches are a two-edged weapon. They add a lot to the price and, if they have been improperly used, they can inflict serious damage to the suspension and chassis. They can also inflict damage on the chappie using them by the way, so check them *very* carefully before operation.

The test drive

The crunch. If the seller baulks at letting you drive, get him to take you out for a spin. Watch what he is doing and note how long it takes to get the brute started. Do a lot of listening as he selects the gears and sets off. A howl from the depths as he finds first means either the clutch release bearing is shot, or your mate is still underneath. When moving off you can expect a bit of noise from first, but from then on the gearbox should be silent apart from a slight whining. It is after all a large and fairly robust bit of kit, and will make quite a lot of noise as speed builds up. Any loud clonks on the take-up of drive, or when going into overrun, means serious wear in the gearbox, the transfer box or the driveline. Get the man to accelerate in each gear and then lift off quite sharply, with his mitt well away from the gear lever. This should show up any gear – particularly second or third – that has developed the habit of jumping out of mesh. A similar test in four-wheel drive and low ratio should be requested, and keep a sharp lookout for any reluctance of four-wheel drive to disengage. That's the yellow knob which should pop up when low ratio (red) is pulled to the rear.

Get the man to park the vehicle on a nice steep slope, set the parking brake, and then take his foot off the brake pedal. Some cheat so be vigilant. It should hold on any fair slope and not come off with a 'bonk' when released.

As the vehicle progresses along the road, observe how the various patterns of road surface affect the steering. A little weaving which is self-correcting (without too much driver input) is acceptable, but if a moderate pot-hole or rut results in a big kick at the wheel ask the man why this is. He should say that the steering and swivel damping is a little slack, as well as calling down a curse on the local highway authority. Beware of wheel wobble at any speed. Land Rover wheels and tyres are big, and correcting any imbalance on such a wheel would take enough lead to line a fall-out shelter. More likely a buckled wheel is the culprit, or a split tyre repaired with a great big truck gaiter.

Ask for a demonstration of braking on the road and brace yourself, remembering that any fluid leaks might provoke an untidy pirouette in the road. This is guaranteed to set a copper's pulse rate up, and they are always around for this sort of thing!

Cross country demonstrations are not as essential as one might think because the vehicle will function just as well on the road as it will in the field. Besides, a lot of guys think they are much better in the rough than they really are, and this can lead to problems. Freed from the restraint of normal road laws and keen to show his worth, our man might just overdo things and stuff it badly. Now I just love and admire doctors and nurses, but I prefer to meet them in pubs rather than in casualty departments. And I bet you paid no heed to your mother's advice to change out of your raggy vest in case you had an accident.

After a run of about three or four miles you should have formed an opinion as to whether the Land Rover can be sorted out and is within the scope of your bag of gold, or whether it's a load of rubbish and should be left well alone. So, we move on to the most fraught task of all, finally making up your mind.

Final considerations

Thank the bemused vendor for his patience, and politely ask him if you and your partner in crime could confer for a few minutes. A *real* Land Rover man will regale you with tea and buns on an upturned pail in his garage. Never in the house, because if you did your checkover at all well you will be filthy. He will then leave you alone until you have decided.

BUYING A USED 4WD VEHICLE

Go over all you have seen, and put an approximate price on any repairs or replacements that will have to be done before the vehicle is up to scratch (or the MOT), and subtract this from the cash you have in hand. Then take away half as much again, because you are bound to discover even more problems later. If you have now arrived at a minus figure, go and tell the man as nicely as possible that the vehicle is not for you and depart, thanking him for his time.

If you are still in the game, do not simply accept the seller's first price. I love haggling for cars and so might he. Point out what in your view will need to be done to the vehicle in the immediate future, and ask him what sort of sum he was realistically looking for. If he comes up with a price that looks like a complete steal, you suddenly have a Land Rover. If not, and you are sure that the vehicle is the one for you, then gently open the process of negotiation. Coming on too strong will only make the target dig his toes in, so 'softly, softly catchee monkey' is the way to proceed. Suggest a figure low enough to be added to as concessions are made, but not so low as to insult him. Do not be encouraged by the offer of a year's MOT certificate, because there are still those who test by post. Take his offer of a test, but ask for it to be conducted at a garage of your choosing. Some sellers, when attention is drawn to the tyres on the vehicle, will suddenly produce a much better set from the back of a shed. The same applies to seats and soft tops. Funny that!

In the final analysis, the price you pay is up to you and your supporting cast. The seller cannot avoid being impressed by the careful way in which you have inspected the vehicle, and (we hope) by your politeness. He will certainly want to sell to you if possible, so work out a deal for yourself.

A useful move is to tell the man that you will pay for the vehicle when he delivers it to your premises. This can solve problems of insurance and lets him take the rap if there is anything illegal on the vehicle that attracts the attention of the law. Now you have the vehicle in your clutches and if you find that any monkey business has been going on, you can stop the cheque or post-date it if you like. Your local Citizens Advice Bureau can run a check to see if the vehicle is subject to an HP agreement.

Have a receipt ready for the man. Something like: 'Received from Joe Bloggs of 23 High Street, Anywhere, the sum of £... as sole payment for Land Rover, vehicle reg. no. XXX XXX, which is my property and not subject to any let or lien'. Get someone to witness this, and keep a copy.

So now you own a Land Rover. You have told your loved one how useful it will be, the kids have climbed on the roof and are playing at being Rommel, and the thing is filling your driveway to the exclusion of all else. For the love of pity don't go berserk. Get to know your new chariot gradually and learn to live with its little ways, like its thirst, its love affair with the nearside kerb of every cambered road, and the sheer joy of driving head and shoulders above every saloon car in the world.

If you begin to have second thoughts when actually faced with your potential purchase, remember that this is what it's all about – off-road enjoyment. (Photo: Chris Bennett).

3
Learning to live with a 4WD

Again from Jim Bradley, this chapter is adapted from an article that first appeared in Overlander 4 × 4 *magazine. It forms a companion piece to his valuable notes on buying a Land Rover.*

During the course of the previous chapter we followed the progress of an off-road pilgrim as he set about the task of selecting his first Land Rover. The natural progression from this is a period of time which sees the new owner adapting himself, his family and his friends, to a completely different way of getting around.

We join our hero in his driveway. He has *the* machine on his own patch at last. It's all his, and life for the moment is good. Poor dope! Little does he realize that a great deal lies ahead before he can think of driving his new chariot with anything like normal peace of mind. He must learn to handle it in the style necessary for a vehicle which weighs as much as a small Rolls-Royce, and has the ride and performance of a small truck. He must learn to look after it, and become conversant with all the odd knocks and rattles which will tell him – if he listens attentively enough – that he will soon be required to mend something.

Learning to live with a Land Rover is a process of constant adjustment, of trying to forget everything you ever knew about 'ordinary' cars. Take the seating plan for instance. Now this is more important than you think. It's no problem for you, the driver, because you are assured of a seat all to yourself, but think of the passengers. It is definitely bad practice to cram the back of the vehicle with bods who have to perch on wheel boxes or old tyres, which might make an efficient seat for short trips, but soon become very tiresome. Try to arrange things so that every person who travels with you has a proper seat which is firmly fastened to the vehicle. Everyone should also have at least a foot of headroom, and be adjacent to an exit which can be opened from the inside.

Children are a different matter again when it comes to seating. They should all have seats in which they can be firmly fastened for their own safety, because even a low-speed emergency stop can lead to very severe injuries if they come adrift. Just consider the amount of hard, unyielding metal surfaces and edges that make up the interior of most 4WD vehicles! The mathematicians among you can work out the kinetic energy produced by a 40 lb infant when the vehicle stops from 25 mph in about 30 ft. A child who is being constantly jolted about in a car is also twice as likely to part company with his last meal as one who is firmly supported, which seems to me another splendid reason why the kiddies should belt up.

So, assuming everyone is comfortably and safely seated, the time has come for a brief shakedown journey. Think in terms of a circular trip around the locality, so if anything drastic goes wrong, getting home will be less of a bind. Remember that when you had your Mini (or whatever) a fiver's worth of petrol went a long way. Not so with a Land Rover: you would be well advised to estimate consumption at well under 20 mpg unless you have a very light foot, at least until you get to know the vehicle better. During your drive try to identify the various noises you will hear in a vehicle with virtually no soundproofing, so that you can investigate the more worrying ones when you get a chance.

Servicing

Providing you are happy so far, the next decisions to be taken are related to servicing work. To carry out any servicing or repairs to the Land Rover (or any similar vehicle), you will need a selection of tools.

Any competent mechanic will be able to give you an idea of what is necessary. Do not go out and buy one of the much vaunted 'complete' tool kits; they are usually poor value for money, and are often padded out with tools you would only need to overhaul a jump jet. Far better to think out in advance what you will be doing, and buy tools for the job. A little tip here is that the official Land Rover workshop manual (the bible) very considerately precedes each job instruction with a note of the tools required. Isn't that nice of them.

Many of your aunties and other bits of the family are not the most imaginative of gift buyers at birthdays and Christmas. Now it may seem a bit cheeky, but it might be wise to circulate a list of tool needs along with a rough price guide to help them in their deliberations. No kidding, it really does work, even though you will have to buy your own socks for a few years.

No job other than the most trivial should be attempted without having recourse to a workshop manual. The version issued by the maker of your vehicle has to be the best, although many of the others, notably the Autobooks range, are well worth consideration.

A hydraulic jack of about two tons capacity is a very desirable addition to your equipment. The choice of a trolley or bottle jack is yours, although I prefer the bottle type because they can also be used as a makeshift press in some circumstances. A pair (or better still, two pairs) of axle stands are also a big help. Axle stands are more important than a lot of people realize, because a Land Rover, even a small one, tips the scales at about the 28 cwt mark. If you are underneath and it falls off the jack it will probably kill you – not necessarily by squashing you flat, but by squeezing you just enough to stop you breathing or crying for help. So never, even for a few seconds, work under a vehicle solely supported by a jack. Even a sideways gust of wind can topple a Land Rover off a jack without any warning, all too frequently with fatal results. If you have no axle stands then wood blocks are acceptable, providing they are of railway-sleeper proportions. *Do not use bricks because they will crush to bits and kill you!* Also remember that the Land Rover has a transmission handbrake, so chocks on the front and rear surfaces of each grounded wheel are essential.

A cursory look under the vehicle will tell you that you are going to need something other than your best bird-pulling gear in order to do very much in the way of work. Any maintenance work on a motor vehicle involves a certain amount of dirt, but Land Rovers really are top of the 'mucky-motors' league. Most of what you lever out of the nooks and crannies of the wheel arches will be a slightly greasy version of the stuff you need for a good crop of potatoes, so its presence on the living-room carpet will leave the lady of the house distinctly underwhelmed. If you want to live in peace, get some kit for the job. At least two boiler suits (not the nylon variety), nice and big for freedom of movement and the inevitable shrinkage in the wash. Work gloves, although too clumsy for ordinary jobs, can be a big help for operations like exhaust replacement, undersealing or chassis cleaning. Also, unless you are into regular Gunk shampoos, an ex-military anti-flash hood like the ones you saw on all those Falklands war TV programmes can be obtained from a lot of surplus stores.

Of all the articles I recommend for your well-being while you tackle the mechanical work, this last item is the most important of all. I don't give a damn if you emerge from underneath your treasured chariot with your only good pair of jeans as black as a blind cobbler's thumb, but I do care about keeping your eyes in good condition. *Always, always*, make sure that for any operations on the underside of the vehicle, or for anything which involves grinding, hammer work, spraying or similar, you wear a pair of goggles. Not safety spectacles – they are useless unless you are vertical all the time – but goggles. The only type really recommended are those that carry an appropriate British Standards Institute (BSI) approval mark, designed specifically for use with grinding wheels. You can rapidly recover from a hammered thumb, a fair old gash or a bit of a burn, but I have the best qualifications in the world to tell you that very little eye damage will put you out of the game for a long, long time, during which you will undoubtedly learn how to suffer.

Now that we have got through the sermon bit, let's assume that you are going to carry out some task on the vehicle. Get it set in your mind exactly what it is you want to do (a check on all oil levels, for instance) and stick to that job all the way. If you see something else that needs attention, note it and return to the problem once you have completed your original task. If you do not, you will get into an

FOUR WHEEL DRIVING

Mercedes-Benz 300GD (or 300GE) for relatively luxurious off-roading – or for cruising down to the marina.

The V6 Mitsubishi Shogun is one of the few petrol-engined off-road vehicles available with a choice of manual or automatic gearbox.

Appropriately named after a sure-footed mountain goat, the Ibex is a Land Rover/Range Rover-based specialist off-road vehicle. The big 'balloon' tyres greatly improve its traction on soft, boggy surfaces.

LEARNING TO LIVE WITH A 4WD

Toyota Landcruiser VX; a good combination of diesel engine and automatic gearbox.

The Isuzu Trooper is available in three- or five-door versions, with either a fuel-injected petrol engine or a turbocharged diesel. The transmission system includes a five-speed manual gearbox and part-time four-wheel drive.

The lively Suzuki Vitara is one of the smallest standard off-road vehicles.

FOUR WHEEL DRIVING

awful muddle and miss important parts of the work. Before starting any job, open the good book to the right pages and put the whole thing into a clear polythene bag so that you see the instructions without getting your mucky paws all over those nice diagrams. Ideally the bag should be large enough to enable you to turn the pages with the book still inside.

A plan I use myself is based on preventative maintenance. Rather than trying to complete a full service in one go, I break the work up into sessions where I concentrate on a particulr part of the vehicle. I usually start with the engine, checking plugs, points, tappets, a general visual inspection of fan belts, hoses, wires, fuel lines and control linkages. A spanner check on all accessible nuts and fasteners is good policy. The next session will be oil levels and greasing, with a visual check of the general under area. If things have gone well and time is available, brakes are next, with a close inspection of tyre treads and sidewalls for cuts and bulges while the wheels are off. Work done in this methodical way can reveal a potentially expensive defect at an early stage, and such things can often be put right before they cost you a big bag of gold.

The electrical system

This is one of the most dreaded sectors of any vehicle maintenance plan. By and large this dread is well earned, because most people tend to neglect or abuse the system, despite its obvious importance. Land Rover wiring tends to be a law unto itself, with looms disappearing into the chassis near the bulkhead, only to emerge at the back into a real nest of connectors and cables that are often further complicated by wires to a badly installed trailer socket. On older vehicles the colour coding will be too faded to be of any use, so the only way of tracing a circuit needs a test-lamp and a fire extinguisher. If you intend to do anything whatsoever to the wiring, always disconnect the battery first. Then, if you have made a mistake which produces a short, you are in just the right place to whip off a clamp to prevent a really good blaze from starting.

Diesel

I must not forget our friends in the diesel sector of the market. A sizeable number of Land Rover owners run and enjoy the diesel-engined models. They are, by and large, quite reliable, although a lot noisier. A new owner with a diesel model would be very well advised to start his ownership with a thorough clean-out of the fuel tank, the sediment bowl (if fitted), and the replacement of the fuel filters. The odds are ten to one that the engine will resemble a black blob on more senior examples of the breed, and a good steam-cleaning is money well spent so you can see where all the oil is coming from. Don't be alarmed by modest leakages of fuel from various points. These can usually be cured by new joint washers at the unions, or by replacing some of the low-pressure supply and return piping.

By far the most important matter for the diesel man is careful maintenance of the heater plug system. It's a bit frail at the best of times, and in the winter the engine just refuses to start without a lengthy burst of heat, so check that the plugs work, and that the resistor coil on the bulkhead does not look too cooked. The other big must for a diesel engine is the provision of a tip-top battery. These are not cheap and have a relatively short life. Unless you have lots of amps in hand on a frosty morning always park on a slope. Should you be fortunate enough to have a garage for your diesel Land Rover, an immersion heater that fits into the cooling system is a useful accessory. These keep the water warm overnight and remove most of the normal starting problems. If you are a real electrical genius, you could arrange for the heater to switch itself on three hours or so before you normally set off in the morning. A nightly trickle charge is also a good idea.

Now that we have trodden this far along the path of the newcomer to the off-road scene, we will inevitably have reached a parting of the ways. Some will have got it bad, and their conversation will be heavy with references to high and low boxes, diff locks and the like. They will be penniless, happy among their new found friends, and yearn for snowy mornings so they can be king of the street. Others, to whom we must extend our deepest sympathy, will have sat down in a darkened room with pen, paper and bank statement to hand, and written the last testament to a bygone pleasure, 'For Sale, SWB Land Rover, petrol, good condition, genuine reason for sale, offers please to ...'.

'Many are called – few are chosen.'

LEARNING TO LIVE WITH A 4WD

LEFT
Long-wheel-base, short-wheel-base – the latter on 'active service' with the National Park Wardens, Peak District. (Photo: Dennis Baldry).

BELOW
An immaculate Land Rover Defender starts to lose its wax finish; 13 Defender 110 TDi's accompanied the Discoverys as backup vehicles on the 1991 Camel Trophy expedition – see Chapter 12. (Photo: Chris Bennett).

4
Off-road driving

Before you venture off the tarmac to start playing in the mud it is essential that you understand something about the handling characteristics of your new toy.

All cross-country vehicles have substantially more ground clearance than a conventional car, and the suspension systems need to be longer to allow for a much greater freedom of movement. The passenger compartment therefore has to be mounted well above most of the working machinery, which results in a much taller, slightly less stable vehicle. This is not a fault in design, but simply a reflection of the design requirement.

The additional height of the vehicle obviously raises its centre of gravity, and the longer suspension travel increases its capacity to roll. The combination makes the whole thing far more likely to corner poorly, and even roll over completely if pushed too hard. Most of these vehicles corner like a China Clipper under full sail, even at quite moderate speeds, and any attempt to emulate the local whizz-kid in his 16-valve GTi turbo-hatchback will almost certainly ruin your day. Remember that any vehicle is only as capable as its driver, and if you want to play silly games on corners join the whizz-kids of this world. If you would rather play silly games in the mud – which is much more fun anyway – you will have to accept certain limitations on your road driving.

The art of successful off-road driving is concerned with careful preparation and reasonable anticipation of what lies ahead. As part of the preparation it is important to remove anything from underneath the bumpers that might impede the vehicle's approach and departure angles; this includes fog and reversing lights, number plates and, if possible, towbars – anything in fact that might get broken off or cause the vehicle to get hung up.

Now open the bonnet and the boot or back door. Is the battery secured with a good clamp to stop it flying about if you have the misfortune to roll? Battery acid will leave an engine looking decidedly past it, and it can be great fun to clear up! If your battery does not have a clamp, get one before you even think about going off-road. Inside the vehicle everything should be stowed and secure, ideally tied or bolted down. Having half a ton of jack or a big tool box trying to join you in the front seat is a guaranteed way of collecting a very expensive headache – especially if everything starts moving when you're half way down a bumpy 45 degree slope. If it isn't necessary to carry something, remove it before you start. If it is necessary, then secure it safely.

By now you should have a pile of assorted junk sitting by your vehicle, and you are almost ready to go. Before you do, walk round to the front and look at the big lump of metal that consumes all your hard-earned cash, and check that you remembered to waterproof it. If you own a diesel you will have no problems, but if you have a petrol engine you will need to run riot with some form of waterproofing agent such as WD40, good old grease or even spray-on insulation foam (yes, I have seen it used!). You will certainly need to completely seal the distributor, high-tension leads and spark plugs, but while you are running amok under the bonnet you might as well have a go at the alternator and any other electrical goodies. If you decide to use the spray-on foam, for goodness sake make sure that everything is in working order before you swamp it in gunge, because the stuff is a nightmare to remove.

First Outing

After paying a local urchin sufficient protection money to mind your pile of junk, climb into the

OFF-ROAD DRIVING

vehicle and prepare to disappear over the horizon on your first cross-country drive. Grasp the steering wheel with a fair degree of determination, but remove your thumbs from inside the rim. This is a difficult thing to remember but it is important, because if you hit a rock or something similar, the wheel will flick back on your thumbs and in all likelihood, break them. You will only need to do it once!

Nicely controlled off-road driving is only possible if you use the transmission system correctly, with nearly all the work being done by the gearbox and very little by the brakes. The best way of learning this technique is to find a spare field (with the owner's consent) or rough track and have a play. Remember to lock your freewheel hubs if the vehicle has manual ones. These should really be checked every time before you select four-wheel drive, because if you forget them you will certainly come to an ignominious halt at the first mud hole. If your vehicle is fitted with permanent four-wheel drive, now is the time to engage the differential lock.

You will already know that you are the proud owner of two gear levers. The lever for the main gearbox will normally be kept in second or third gear for most off-road driving, with occasional forays into first for all steep descents. The small lever is in command of the transfer box, and is used for the selection of high and low range, and for the engagement of four-wheel drive.

Try to familiarize yourself with the range of available gear ratios. Engage low range in third gear and trot around for a while, and if there are any gentle hills and slopes, trundle up and down to get the feel of how the engine pulls and what effect engine-braking has. Avoid anything too adventurous in the way of hills at this stage, and do not, under any circumstances, attempt to turn round on a hillside unless you want to roll the vehicle over!

After trying a similar exercise in second gear, change down into first and notice how incredibly low this gearing is. On most vehicles the ratio will be about 47:1, which will give you safe engine-braking down the steepest of driveable slopes. In most cases it would be much quicker to walk.

Now try to find some mild undulations to give yourself an idea of how the soft, long-travel suspension reacts, and what sort of feel it imparts to the

Before you go off-road driving, remove everything you can from beneath the front and rear bumpers. Having already dispensed with the tow hook, the author is seen here removing the bumper side cappings.

FOUR WHEEL DRIVING

ABOVE
The two gear levers control the main and transfer boxes.

RIGHT
The axle differentials are generally the lowest point on any off-road vehicle, and knowing where they are in relation to any obstruction could be important.

vehicle. You will also need to familiarize yourself with the importance of ground clearance. The lowest points of any off-road vehicle are generally the axle differentials, and although you can't see them from the cab, it will be vital to understand where they are and what effect they could have on your continued mobility.

Off into the rough stuff

After a gentle introduction to the vehicle and its off-road capabilities, you will probably be itching to get away into some real rough stuff. Before you do, it would be as well to reflect on some of the conditions you are likely to meet, and learn the commonsense techniques for dealing with them.

Steep ascents: The primary rule for tackling any steep hill is always go up or down with your vehicle at right angles to the slope: if you turn sideways across the gradient you will dramatically increase the risk of a rollover. Park the vehicle at the bottom of the slope so that you can go straight up, and engage third gear in low range (or second if you have a diesel). Now accelerate slowly, using just enough power to keep the vehicle moving, but not enough to bounce you all over the place or lose your precious grip. You must try to keep the wheels on the ground at all times or you will lose traction. If the vehicle starts labouring, accelerate slightly until it feels comfortable again.

Some hills will be so steep that all you can see ahead is the vehicle's bonnet and the wide open sky. If this happens, you will have to rely on feel to tell you when the front wheels have crested the top, and then back-off the accelerator quickly and park the vehicle away from the slope. Always leave it in gear and with the ignition switched off – particularly if you have recently been wading because the handbrake may be wet and fail to hold the vehicle.

Never attempt to climb any slope if it looks steeper than 45 degrees.

Aborted ascents: Sooner or later you will find yourself in the unenviable position of having to stop half way up a slope, because the vehicle simply will not make it to the top.

If the engine has actually stalled through lack of power, put your foot on the brake pedal (*keeping your other one off the clutch*) before you start rolling back down the slope, and keep it there. Do not rely on the handbrake in this situation because it probably won't hold you. Switch off the ignition and take a couple of seconds to breathe deeply and reflect on your position.

Now what can you do? You cannot go forwards because you don't have the power, so you will have to reverse down the slope under engine-braking. Keeping your right foot on the brake, dip the clutch and select reverse gear. Now move you left foot away from the pedals, and keep it away! You are now all set to go straight back down the hill, but first you need to start the engine on the key – and timing is important here.

Turn the ignition, and as soon as the engine fires lift your foot gently off the brake, but be prepared to put it back on again if the gear lever is not fully engaged or jumps out. As soon as you feel the gearbox safely engaged, take your foot away from the brakes and don't touch any of the pedals until you arrive at the bottom. The low range gearing will ensure that you descend in absolute safety.

If you decide half way up a slope that you are not going to make it, the technique is basically the same except that the engine is still running and you don't have the luxury of a few moments to gather yourself. As soon as you decide to reverse, apply the footbrake to prevent the vehicle rolling backwards, select reverse gear in the normal way, and release the brake as soon as the clutch is fully engaged. You will then descend in full control all the way.

You must keep your feet clear of all the pedals throughout the actual descent. Braking is very tempting on occasions, but if you lose grip on a loose surface the vehicle will slide down the hill and accelerate quite quickly. If you disengage the clutch you will freewheel down and accelerate *very* quickly; and we all know what happens if you play with the other pedal!

If you are in an automatic vehicle everything is a lot easier. Simply plant your right foot on the brake, slide the selector into reverse, release the brake and away you go.

The first time you try any of these manoeuvres you will undoubtedly feel a little unsure of yourself. Don't be – remember what it was like when you first learned to drive? I taught myself these skills on a very steep country lane before venturing off-road, so if I fluffed it I could still brake safely. Practise, and practise again, until you feel confident.

FOUR WHEEL DRIVING

A word of warning. Do not attempt to climb any steep slope unless you are absolutely sure there is a plateau at the top – or at least room to stop the vehicle. These slopes can lead straight to a vertical drop into a disused quarry or over a cliff, so always check on foot before you drive anywhere.

Steep descents: The secret of a safe descent is to use engine compression to hold the vehicle back – braking it all the way down the slope. The wheel brakes should never be touched on a steep, loose surface, because the soil will move, the wheels will lock, the back end of the vehicle will attempt to overtake the front and you will end up rolling over.

To descend under full control, align the vehicle at 90 degrees to the lip of the slope and engage first gear in low range. Accelerate very slightly, just enough to get moving, and as soon as you feel the front wheels go over the lip, take both feet away from all pedals and let the engine do the work: the gearing will restrict your speed to less than walking pace, and you will arrive at the bottom in complete safety.

ABOVE
Some hills are so steep that you can see nothing ahead but the vehicle's bonnet and the sky. There are no road-signs in this sort of terrain, so you must check on foot before you reach the top of anything like this. It could lead you straight into a quarry. (Photo: *Off Road & 4 Wheel Drive magazine*)

RIGHT
Stalled on a steep hill. Now what do you do?

Never use the brake or clutch pedals at any time during a steep descent, or you will arrive at the bottom out of control and probably in need of an ambulance.

You may find that the engine braking is so powerful that the back of the vehicle starts to skid out. If this occurs you must go against all your natural inclinations and accelerate very slightly – just enough to pull the back end into line again. As soon as the vehicle has straightened up, abandon the

36

throttle pedal and let gravity do the rest. This is a fairly common problem with the very high compression ratio diesels, and the procedure is completely safe providing you feed the power in gently.

Camel humps: These delightful little hills have a steep upslope and a steep downslope, with very little in between – exactly like a camel's hump in fact! If you are blessed with a good sense of balance you will find them no problem, but if like me you lack this natural equilibrium life can be very interesting. Ascend the upslope in second or third gear, just as you would on any other steep hill. As the vehicle starts to roll over the top, you will need to engage the lowest possible gear to give you maximum engine-braking for the downward journey. This is where your sense of balance comes in useful. The change needs to be at just the right point, otherwise you can stall the vehicle; use too much power and break your grip; or even hurtle down the slope in neutral.

Driving in ruts: The natural temptation when driving off-road is to follow the ruts left by other vehicles. This is a pretty dumb thing to do unless you are absolutely sure of your ground. The ruts could have been made by countless tractor journeys or a squadron of Her Majesty's tanks, in which case they will be much deeper than your ground clearance and you could end up firmly lodged on the central ridge.

The grassy edges and centre always look tempting, but they often conceal such delights as rusty wire (great for punctures), disused agricultural implements or bits of old angle-iron. Nevertheless, the safest way forward is probably to straddle the ruts, with one wheel on the nearside verge and the other on the ridge, but you must travel slowly and keep a sharp eye open for possible obstructions.

If you really have no alternative to driving in the ruts themselves, remember that anticipation is vital. If you lose concentration, you may find that the furrows gradually become deeper until the vehicle grounds itself and becomes well and truly stuck. This is known as being 'high-centred', and usually involves a lot of digging, winching, towing and swearing to get you 'un-high centred'. Forward momentum can often be restored in an hour or so, but your dignity might take a little longer to recover.

Crossing ruts: The technique here is to keep all four wheels firmly on the ground at all times, to achieve

FOUR WHEEL DRIVING

As soon as you feel the front wheels go over the lip, take both feet away from the pedals and let engine-braking do all the work.

maximum traction and reduce the amount of effort needed from the vehicle.

Engage first gear if the ruts are hard and dry, or second gear if everything is slippery. Aim the vehicle to cross the line of the ruts at about 30 degrees, and drive very slowly through, feeding in enough power to overcome the resistance, but not so much that you spray mud or dust in all directions. Always ensure that only one wheel is in a rut at any one time, or you may end up being 'cross-axled' – a delightfully descriptive condition that has enormous entertainment value for the onlookers. This occurs when you get the angles all wrong and drop diagonally opposite wheels into ruts at the same time, leaving the other two on firm ground but with nothing to push against. All traction is lost and you grind to a halt until someone arrives with a tow-rope. If you get the angles right, the vehicle will clamber through the obstruction like a wise old tortoise.

Never attempt to cross ruts at right-angles. The amount of power needed to pull even one wheel out of a rut is surprisingly high, but if you drop both front wheels in at the same time you will probably find the resistance is far too high for you to gain any traction – particularly if the ground is very loose or slippery.

Fording a river or stream: Just because the water comes only half-way up the ducks, is no guarantee that it will be shallow enough for you to drive through. When you come to a ford or river crossing stop, switch off and have a good look at the entry and exit angles. Check the current and apparent depth of the water, and look for any obstacles that could impale themselves on the underside of your vehicle.

An area of calm water can often be a sign that a gaping chasm lurks beneath the surface, while a ripple can indicate the presence of submerged rocks or an old bike (imagine that tangled round your drive shafts). Check to see if the crossing is used frequently, and if it is, whether a clear route has been established. If your vehicle is destined for a lengthy paddle, make sure that any necessary wading plug is inserted in the transmission.

Enter the water slowly and in low gear, and drive calmly but steadily across. The bow-wave at the front of the vehicle should have a slight hollow around the engine area. If it looks as though the

OFF-ROAD DRIVING

Even authors get it all wrong sometimes! Cross-axled in Scotland after trying (unsuccessfully) to clamber out of deep ruts. Notice the left front and right rear wheels. The problem was finally resolved by going into reverse and finding another exit route – but more often than not this is a tow-rope job!

water is getting too deep, always go back – particularly if even a moderate current is running. Any depth of water that begins to worry you will almost certainly have the power to push the vehicle over. Never wear seat belts in fast running water, just in case you have to exit the vehicle quickly.

Do not enter the water at high speed. It may impress your friends as you spray several hundred gallons of the stuff all over the place, but they will not be too chuffed about getting their feet wet while trying to push you and your dead vehicle out of the river.

Assuming you reach the other side in complete safety, stop the vehicle and let it tick over for a while so that the heat and the fan can dry out all the electrical bits. When you do finally drive off, hold your foot lightly on the brake pedal for a few minutes to allow friction to dry the brakes – particularly if the vehicle has drum brakes.

Always remember that a shallow river can very quickly turn into a dangerous, raging torrent following heavy rain on nearby hills.

Crossing side slopes: Nice diagrams in glossy brochures will tell you that most 4WD vehicles can traverse a side slope of about 35 degrees without falling over, but that does not necessarily mean that you should attempt to get anywhere near that figure. All manner of things can change the apparent centre of gravity of a moving vehicle, suddenly converting an interesting drive into a highly dangerous situation. Undulating ground is part of the very nature of cross-country driving, and bumps and hollows in an otherwise flat field can often rock a vehicle from one side to the other by 15-20 degrees without you really noticing. These undulations are just as prevalent on the side of any hill, and dropping the downslope wheel into a rabbit burrow or hitting a largish rock on the upslope side can topple you over in an instant. Even if the theoretical centre of gravity limit has not been reached,

FOUR WHEEL DRIVING

Always drive slowly in water, use a low gear and keep a sharp look-out for rocks and hollows. (Photo: *Chris Bennett*)

momentum will often do the rest – especially when all your passengers, picnic gear, jack and toolboxes lurch over to the downhill side of the vehicle together and give it a hefty thump. For similar reasons, wet grass and loose ground can be particular hazards on a traverse: if the vehicle begins to slide sideways down even a quite moderate slope, the momentum can easily be transferred into a rolling motion if the wheels hit a big tuffet say, or a tree stump.

Clearly side slopes are dangerous and should be treated with the utmost caution and respect. They have a nasty habit of suddenly getting steeper halfway across, and before you know it, you're in acute danger of rolling over. If you find yourself in this situation remove everyone from the vehicle and take a few deep breaths. Can you carry on, or will the vehicle roll over if you do? Unless you have absolute confidence in your ability, you must start looking for escape routes. Ideally try to retrace your steps to get the vehicle back out of danger, but if that is not possible, and you are past the worst, a few minutes work with your trusty spade might restore the situation. If you feel at any time that the vehicle is going to topple over, steer downhill immediately and rethink your strategy.

Unless you really have to traverse a steep side slope, they are better avoided altogether.

Stopping on a downhill slope: This can be done in exceptional circumstances (if someone has an accident in front of you for instance), but do not lunge for the brake pedal or you will lock all the wheels, and on a loose or wet surface you will slide or roll all the way to the bottom.

If you are descending correctly in first gear and with your feet off the pedals, all you need do is turn off the ignition. As simple as that! Because you are moving so slowly anyway, the engine will stop and the vehicle will come to a safe and controlled halt. If it jerks forward slightly, this will be the downhill momentum trying to turn the engine against its compression, which can be stopped by applying *light* pressure on the brakes. When you are ready to re-start, simply take your foot away from the brake pedal, turn the key and away you go.

Driving on snow: A fresh fall of snow can be absolute heaven for a 4WD owner – no wheelspin, no worries about fitting snow chains, and no fear of missing important appointments.

Please be aware, however, that although you can put the power down without the back end looking like a salmon swimming upstream, you will have just as much trouble stopping as ordinary two-wheel drive vehicles. Having power on all four wheels means that the road never *feels* as slippery as it really is – until you try to brake normally, and then you can be like everyone else as you pirouette gracefully down the road.

The techniques for safe driving in the snow are very much the same as those used for normal off-road driving. On soft or packed snow, engage four-wheel drive (or the differential lock on a permanent 4WD system) to give yourself maximum traction while under way; this will also help to reduce the possibility of wheel-locking as you slow down. As with off-road driving, the use of brakes should be kept to a minimum by using the gearbox to reduce speed. Tell following traffic what you intend to do by gently flashing the brake lights, and then leave well alone until you are finally ready to stop. A smooth and gentle application of the brakes should then do the trick.

If you feel unsure about driving in high-range gears on soft snow, engage the low-range and select third – as you would for normal off-road driving. This way you can drive almost entirely on the gearbox, changing down into second for increased engine braking. This technique would also hold good if you deliberately had to enter snow to recover a stuck vehicle or drive round an obstruction.

Whenever snow is around, always keep at least some heat directed onto the windscreen to prevent the wipers from freezing to the glass. As soon as the roads have cleared and everything gets back to normal, head off to your local river or steam-cleaning plant to give the vehicle a good underbelly wash. Accumulated road salt is highly corrosive and does untold damage unless it is removed quickly.

Driving in sand: Although sand invariably looks

The Range Rover can handle quite steep angles on a traverse, but these slopes can be extremely dangerous and should be avoided unless you have a lot of experience.

FOUR WHEEL DRIVING

Perfect weather for 4WD; but remember that although you can put the power down more easily than less fortunate 2WD drivers, conventional braking can be just as embarrassing or dangerous. Use the gears to control speed as much as possible. (Photo: Dennis Baldry).

inviting, it can be highly unpredictable stuff and should be treated with respect. Dry sand can move around under your wheels far more than most surfaces, and it has the capacity to blow into tempting, snow-drift like dunes around rocks that would stop a battle tank. Wet sand relies on the underlying substrate for its stability, and the weight of a vehicle can easily break through weak areas in its deceptively uniform surface.

The most important thing to remember about driving on sand is not to turn the steering wheel too sharply. If you do, the sideloads will build up a barrier of sand on the outside of the driving wheels, which could cause a 'negative momentum situation' – in other words, you could easily get thoroughly stuck. Driving down a sandy hill is not as easy as it looks, because the resistance of sand to forward motion is quite surprising. The best plan is to engage second gear in the low range and drive down fairly positively. A lot of the sand will want to come down with you, and if you have to stop for any reason the loose surface will continue to flow past you and perhaps build up around the wheels. If this happens, you may well find it best to reverse a little so that the vehicle can get a clear run at the obstruction. Never attempt to drive on a side slope of loose sand! Its capacity for movement is amazing, and the miniature avalanche you create will inexorably turn the vehicle over.

Driving on beaches is not recommended at all. Apart from the environmental damage you can do to fragile ecosystems along the coastline, you are very likely to get stuck. By the time you return to your pride and joy with a heavy recovery truck, Mother Nature will have got her revenge by flooding it with highly corrosive salt water. If you really insist on chancing your arm, always keep to the damp area between high and low water marks, and make sure that all the turns are slow and gentle. If you do get stuck, reverse back and try again, keeping the steering angles very small. Steel and aluminium do not have a happy relationship with salt water, and sand makes an excellent grinding paste for all the rotating machinery, so before you go beach riding consider the possibilities of a slowly decomposing vehicle or the hours of mucky effort required to clean it.

Responsible off-road driving

To have confidence in your off-road driving you must become completely familiar with the capabilities of your vehicle and practise as often as possible, extending yourself a little more each time. Do not try to accomplish too much too quickly. You will often find that your nerve gives out long before you overstretch the vehicle – which is entirely normal, and much safer than the reverse situation. A good 4WD vehicle in the right hands is capable of extraordinary feats, but care is needed to build up to your full potential. Luckily a new problem can lurk around every corner and on every hillside, so if your enthusiasm holds, you will never stop learning about off-road driving. Remember never to tackle anything unless you are completely confident of success, and take all the time you need to refine your technique. You are bound to make mistakes, and you will even get stuck from time to time, but you can profit from these situations by carefully analysing what you did wrong and changing your approach to the job next time.

One last thought – perhaps the most important of all. Please be responsible about how and where you use an off-road vehicle. Remember that we are not the owners of the environment but merely hold it in trust for the next generation. Man has already done more than enough damage to the planet, so please take care of it from now on.

Driving in deep ruts can lead to grounding on the central ridge.

5
Off-road competitions

by Bill Jones

Off-road competitions are now far more than just another obscure branch of mainstream motor sport. For thousands of club members they are virtually a way of life, and every weekend you will find 4WD enthusiasts attending events all over the country. The various competitions are great fun to enter and really spectacular to watch, and helping to run an event for your local club is both educational and satisfying. In addition, everyone involved gets at least some useful off-road experience – even if the vehicle concerned is only being used to provide transport for spectators. The informality of club events is offset very slightly by the obvious need for safety regulations, but you are guaranteed a warm welcome wherever you go. Most of the off-road clubs are as much social as competitive.

The competitions themselves range from the simple and totally safe gymkhana, to the full tilt, blood and guts competitive safari. You can become involved at any level that suits you, your family, or your wallet. Most people, including many of the drivers, underestimate the capabilities of a modern 4WD, and are surprised to learn that lots of club events can be entered by virtually standard vehicles, with only the minimum of modification necessary to make sure they comply with the safety rules. At the other end of the competitive scale, specialist cross-country speed machines can eat spare parts, require regular re-bodying and use petrol by the bucketful!

The first step for any budding off-road competitor is to find a club suitable for his needs (see the Appendix at the end of this book). Some organizations only accept certain makes of vehicle. Notable among these is the Association of Rover Clubs (ARC) which, not unreasonably, only allows vehicles of Rover manufacture to compete in its club events. The ARC has groups catering for Rover enthusiasts all over the country, and increasingly there are comparable clubs which allow other makes – or even a combination of makes – to enter. Vehicles used in the toughest open competitions can usually be made up from a variety of makes and parts, but at ARC events all of the component parts of each vehicle must have come from a Rover originally.

For those who want an inexpensive way to compete in off-road speed events, a 4 × 2 buggy-type vehicle – usually built around Volkswagen parts – is the obvious answer. These are highly competitive in the right conditions (preferably dry), and are certainly cheaper to build and use less fuel than any 4WD machine. Being lighter, they are also much easier to transport to and from an event. Most of them are nothing more than a frame incorporating the engine, gearbox and driver, and if you enter speed competitions in such a vehicle you are certainly going to get very wet and muddy from time to time! In fact if you really object to getting dirty, you would be better off considering a different type of motor sport altogether.

Clubs are run by committees, but their events are held together by individual marshals and officials who are all volunteers – giving their own free time

---

ABOVE RIGHT

A well sponsored Range Rover pick-up nicknamed 'Roar Over'. This kind of vehicle probably has a full service crew and all the financial backing it needs, but it can still be beaten handsomely by a bunch of amateurs. Off-road racing is like that!

RIGHT

A typical 4 × 2 buggy-style vehicle will usually be based on Volkswagen components. Drivers in these events can get seriously muddy! (All photos this chapter: Bill Jones)

158
S.B.C. Racing Team
SPONSORED BY
CYRIL G. GROOMBRIDGE
BFGoodrich

22
BFGoodrich

FOUR WHEEL DRIVING

Concours enthusiasts are immensely proud of their beautifully restored vehicles.

with little or no reimbursement of expenses. No competition could be run without these dedicated people, but they all realize that the experience gained by doing the job can have enormous benefits later. Not only do they find out how an event is organized, set out and run, but as marshals they will also have a front-row seat while the event is in progress. Watching other drivers in competitions should be considered a mandatory experience before taking the plunge yourself. Although you will always have your own ideas on preparation and technique, you can't beat watching someone else under pressure, hopefully learning from the way he keeps the vehicle moving over a particularly nasty bit of terrain.

Off-road clubs vary in size from the nationally-based All Wheel Drive Club, to local groups with only a few enthusiasts. The larger ones will have computer-controlled timing equipment for their competitions, as well as event control trucks or trailers. The competitions secretary is responsible for overall event organization, and for the club's equipment. He will have made sure that the land owner has given his consent for the meeting, that a Royal Autombile Club (RAC) event permit has been obtained, that a clerk of the course and marshals have been appointed, that the St John Ambulance people will send a vehicle and crew, and that entry forms have been sent to all club members. The course for each event is generally set out on the day before the meeting by the clerk of the course and his marshals, but extra help is often needed on competition day to operate the start and timing gear for speed events, or to man the individual sections for trials.

Why off-road?

Many people associated with other branches of motor sport are amazed to find that there are never any money prizes involved, despite the large amounts invested in an off-road speed machine. The most an overall or class winner can hope to receive is a small trophy. So what is the attraction of off-road competition? It can be summed up in the well worn and much over used phrase, 'man and machine against the elements'. In no other motor sport does the driver have to be so much in tune with his vehicle if he wants to succeed. He must, for instance, be able to feel what the wheels are doing, and tell when the engine is labouring almost before it happens, and he must certainly know how to use minimum throttle to regain grip if the wheels start to spin. Anyone can learn the theory of off-road driving, but experience must be gained the hard way. Unlike tarmac, every yard of off-road terrain is unique, and there are no rules written down on a tablet of stone that will tell you how to cross it – you simply have to learn for yourself.

Whether you compete on your own or with a co-driver; use a full service crew or a group of friends; or just have the family with you, you are guaranteed a great time. You'll stay fit, too. In trials or competitive safaris it is often vital to walk the course or section first, and just sitting in a 4WD vehicle which is bouncing all over the place is a sure fire way to lose weight. It can also be very tiring heaving nearly a ton and a half of vehicle about when the wheels are stuck in deep mud. Some vehicles now have powered steering, but the stamina required in general for off-road driving has clearly not put off some very successful lady drivers, most notably in trials.

Most clubs are affiliated to the RAC, but some remain totally independent. The one drawback to this situation is that clubs from the different 'sides' are unable to invite each other to co-promote events. Most of the clubs – whether affiliated or not – operate a system of vehicle classes for their trials and competitive safaris (by far the most common types of off-road event), which ensures that nobody gets an unfair advantage, and provides for a number of 'class awards' rather than just one overall winner. The 1989 *ARC Yearbook* lists nine classes for trials and competitive safaris for Land Rovers, but most of the 'allcomer' clubs have reduced the number of classes to six, usually based on the size of the vehicles's engine, the number of driven wheels or the type of suspension.

There are bound to be meetings almost every weekend somewhere in the country, and most clubs regularly organize so-called 'novice' or 'beginners' events. Previous trophy winners are banned from taking the prizes in these competitions, which gives inexperienced drivers or even complete newcomers the chance to win something. Remember that cross-country motor sport need not be expensive. Once you have your vehicle up to the required level of preparation, the events themselves cost only a few pounds to enter, plus a couple of gallons of fuel: if you do your own repairs and servicing, so much the better. Secondhand spares and special tools can often be picked up cheaply from other club members, who will also be a constant source of advice and encouragement if you have to tackle a particularly difficult job.

Competitive events

In common with many other sports, off-road driving has a number of different competitive levels to allow for varying degrees of experience. The three major levels are 'non-damaging' competitions, cross-country trials and speed events, but most clubs also organize miscellaneous competitions that are rather more social by nature. At the lowest (easiest) level you may well be able to enter a standard road-going vehicle, but the vastly more

An old master of the art – Colin Cowley at the wheel of a Land Rover 90 makes easy work of an RTV Trial section.

difficult trials and speed events demand many hours of preparation and highly specialized machines. These vehicles are normally trailered to and from a competition site because they are modified far too much to be made road legal, and obviously the risk of damage during a competition is high, leaving the competitor stranded at the end of the day.

'Non-damaging' competitions

Clearly no event can be totally non-damaging – the description entirely relies on the driver, his ability, and to a lesser degree on the attitude of the clerk of the course! However, the events in this section could reasonably be entered in a road-going vehicle without risking any more serious harm than an occasional scratch or broken light lens. Most of these events are designed to encourage club members to get on the first step of the competition ladder without having to spend money on a specially prepared second vehicle. As such, they are ideal for the beginner.

Gymkhana, Treasure Hunt and Orienteering. In common with other branches of motor sport, the club Gymkhana involves tackling a number of tasks using the vehicle. Virtually anything goes, but there is often no particular requirement for a 4WD vehicle. These are great competitions for the family to participate in, and will often be held when the club is organizing a weekend of events at one site. Quite rare, but usually good fun. Likewise the Treasure Hunt, which can be organized by the club although 4WD is again not always necessary. Orienteering by vehicle can also be a lot of fun, but for these events a 4WD is really essential. The competition closely follows the pattern set by the conventional pedestrian sport, and a number of

A Suzuki SJ has a close encounter with one of the trial gates. These vehicles are now challenging Land Rover for supremacy in the 'all-comer' events.

OFF-ROAD COMPETITIONS

tasks have to be completed (or questions answered) after visiting locations found by careful map reading.

Vehicle Concours. Not competitive in the true sense of the word, there are nevertheless a lot of enthusiasts who love to rebuild old vehicles and then display them in all their elegant glory. Usually associated with Land Rover clubs, the Vehicle Concours requires a lot of pure dedication and elbow grease, and the originality of all the parts is just as important as the overall condition of the vehicle. Some 40-year old Series I Land Rovers can be made to look like new with enough care and attention. Not for you unless you have an eye for detail and an awful lot of patience.

Road Taxed Vehicle (or Novice) Non-Damaging Trial. These events are often the backbone of a club's competitions calender and are usually very well attended. More commonly known as the RTV Trial (or with some clubs the Family Vehicle Trial – FVT), the courses are set out so that standard road-going machines can enter without fear of rolling over or doing any serious damage. They present an ideal opportunity to every driver to find out what his vehicle can do, and see just how skilful he is at controlling it. From this competition level onwards, all vehicles will be scrutineered to make sure that they comply with the rules and are safe to enter the event.

All trials consist of a number of sections (usually 10–12) which must be tackled by each driver in turn. Each section can be anything from a few yards to a few hundred yards long, and will be pegged out by using pairs of canes. The object of the trial is to drive through the cane 'gates' without stopping and without touching any of the canes; both offences will incur penalty points. Each gate is sequentially numbered, usually starting at ten and working towards zero at the finish, so the further you drive along a section, the fewer penalty points you will collect. As you pass through the final (zero) gate, you will have 'cleared' that section and received zero penalties – unless of course you have been forced to stop or hit any of the gates on the way. Drivers normally carry an event scorecard which is marked at the end of each section by the marshal, and the person with the least number of penalties at the end of the day is the winner.

Some form of rollover protection is compulsory at CCVT events.

In addition to the basic rules of trialing, variations are sometimes incorporated for particular events. An example of this is called 'the shunt', which allows vehicles over a certain length (usually 100 in. wheelbase) to stop, reverse and restart once on each section without incurring any penalties. The driver may have to tell the marshal in advance where he intends taking the shunt.

Cross country vehicle trials

The same basic rules apply to all trials, but the severity of the individual sections alters significantly as soon as you go beyond the stage of using a road-legal vehicle. Cross country vehicle trials (CCVT) are organized in exactly the same way as RTV and other non-damaging trials, but the terrain is much tougher, and there is a greater degree of risk to both vehicle and driver. Because of this risk the preparations include a number of mandatory safety measures that are not really applicable to road-legal machinery, and although the full specifications vary from club to club, you would be well advised to go

FOUR WHEEL DRIVING

for the highest possible standards. Remember that these events are where off-road drivers really cut their teeth and discover just how far they can push their vehicles. Even a well prepared competition machine can tip over very easily on a steep side slope, and some form of rollover protection (often a full roll cage) is compulsory at every meeting. A glance through the written safety requirements of your own club will demonstrate just how tough some of these events can be.

There are a number of different names for these trials. Some clubs call them CCVTs, while others describe them as Expert or Modified Vehicle Trials. Virtually any vehicle modification is acceptable (except for ARC events where everything has to be Rover based), so you can have limited-slip differentials, locking differentials, aggressive tyres, independently operated rear 'fiddle brakes' and even four-wheel steering. Each club will have different rules, so you will need to check what is allowed with the competitions secretary, who will also tell you which set of competition regulations are in force. The Highland 4 Wheel Drive Club for instance, has a system of continual penalties which allow you to touch a marker but still continue to the end of the section. The Cumbrian Rover Owner's Club uses a

---

You can do an awful lot of damage to a vehicle when it comes back to Earth after a 'yump'. Suspension, axles, swivel housings and chassis can all suffer badly from a poor landing.

---

handicap method of scoring which makes the end result a little bit more open, because the more times you win the more penalty points you carry over into the next event!

The atmosphere at these trials can be electric, and because most of the vehicles are open-topped they allow a fair bit of 'encouraging' banter between spectators and competitors during each section. Any driver who finds himself seriously stuck or embarrassed will instantly be on the receiving end of endless advice from the onlookers, who will be both delighted and amused at his misfortune. On the other hand, there will always be a big round of applause when any driver gets a 'clear' on a very difficult section – and an even bigger one if he manages to turn the vehicle over! If you can't stand laughing at yourself, you had better not enter these events – but if you do join in, you will certainly end up laughing at everyone else!

OFF-ROAD COMPETITIONS

One of the fastest teams in Competitive Safaris throughout the 1970s and 1980s has been Pat Willis and Robbo Aliperti. Believe it or not, this machine started life as a Range Rover.

Speed events

With home-built off-road machines reaching 60–70 mph across country, these are by far the most spectacular events to both watch and enter. The most common speed event is the competitive safari, which could more accurately be described as off-road racing. Other variations are far less common, but they all share an element of driving or tackling set tasks against the clock. Because of the speeds involved all of these events are potentially dangerous, and hence the safety requirements and scrutineers will be that much more stringent. The basic competitions need not cost the earth to enter, but your driving style is likely to dictate how much damage you do to the vehicle, and consequently your overall financial commitment. There will certainly be more preparation required though, with the emphasis very much on the safety of yourself, your crew, the event officials and the spectators. The fee you pay to enter all competitive events largely goes on two things – the cost of hiring the land for the day, and premiums for third-party insurances. In the case of RAC-affiliated clubs, a fee is sent to that organization based on the number of competitors entered in the event. This fee covers any third-party claim for damage from the land owner, and any claim after injury to spectators, but it does not cover the competing drivers, any crew or the club officials – all of whom have to accept this condition by signing-in at the start of an event.

Competitive Safaris. The most popular of all speed competitions. Drivers set off at regular intervals (usually 30–60 sec apart) to drive a course which can range from a few hundred yards to several miles in length. The event resembles a timed rally stage in operation, with a standing start and flying finish. You will find all types of vehicle competing, including some very strange-looking hybrids, but ARC safaris are again restricted to all-Rover vehicles and components. Other clubs allow almost anything to take part providing it meets the required safety standards, but recent years have seen a

FOUR WHEEL DRIVING

RIGHT
A Range Rover – almost in the final stages of being recognizable as such! The vehicle was rebuilt as a buggy using home fabricated body panels.

FAR RIGHT
A capstan winch in use at one of the winch-recovery events organized by the Red Rose Land Rover Club, near Preston.

progressive leaning towards Range Rover-based 'specials'. Drivers choose these vehicles because the Rover V8 engine is light, powerful, plentiful and reasonably cheap. The Range Rover's 100 in. wheelbase has also proved to be the best compromise for off-road work because it helps to reduce the violent pitching-movement experienced with shorter vehicles, while maintaining its agility and good obstacle clearance on rough terrain.

The drivers have to attempt the course a certain number of times during the day, and within a pre-arranged time limit. Many clubs now do one lap at a time to reduce the risk of collision between faster and slower vehicles: the laps still have to be driven as quickly as possible, but the race is against the clock, rather than against another vehicle. If anyone takes too long on the course, or breaks down before the finish, he will be given a 'maximum' by the officials. The maximum time penalty can also be given out as a punishment for cutting corners or similar offences – although it is very rare for such penalties to be given in off-road competition because everyone is there to enjoy themselves and deliberate cheating is pointless.

The number of competitors entered in a safari event will very much depend on the size of the club. The smaller clubs may only have a handful of members with safari-type vehicles, whereas the AWDC might expect up to 100 entrants for a single event. If you intend racing with one of the larger organizations it makes a lot of sense to enter one or two smaller, local events first, so that you know what to expect. Most clubs send out entry forms for each event together with any Additional Supplementary Regulations (ASRs) that may apply. These are the club's own rules over and above the RAC's Standing Supplementary Regulations (SSRs), which govern the sport as a whole. You would normally be expected to send off the entry form with your fee before the event, but some clubs allow entries to be accepted on the day. Carry your driving licence and club membership card to all events, because you will need to show them before your entry can be accepted.

Timed Trial. These are very rare nowadays because the vehicles have to be prepared to almost the same standard required for competitive safaris. The sections are similar to normal trials, but drivers are usually allowed to stop, and touching a marker cane does not attract the same penalty. The vehicles are timed through each section and the winner is the driver with the fastest overall time at the end of the day. Each section will be fairly short, and probably less severe than normal.

Team Recoveries. A particularly severe course is laid out, in such a way that it is impossible for one vehicle to drive it unassisted. Teams are formed from the entrants, and they have to drive through various marked obstacles, towing, winching and pushing each other as necessary. The vehicles can leave the direct route of the course to assist another team member, but all the drivers must pass each of the obstacles. The teams are given time at the start to inspect the course, or individual sections of it if appropriate, and each run is timed as a complete team effort after the last vehicle passes the finishing line. Some clubs allow a passenger (or ropeman) to be carried, while others only allow the drivers. These events really do test teamwork, physical stamina, driving skill and recovery techniques to the extreme, and there are *still* drivers who enjoy the challenge! Many clubs, incidentally, require a strong mesh to be fitted over the windscreen and behind the cab as a protection against tow-rope failure.

Point-to-point. These are really a cross-over from horse riding events, and as far as I know they are only organized in the UK by the Pennine Land Rover Club. The course consists of as many as 20 gates similar to those used in trials, set out over many acres of ground. Each team has to drive through all the gates – usually in a specific order – as quickly as possible within a given time limit. If they complete all the gates inside the specified time, they return to control for another scorecard and set off again. Some of the gates will be driveable, but others will need considerable teamwork to get through. A marshall signs the scorecard after he is satisfied that each gate has been driven successfully. Most vehicles will have a crew of two, including the ropeman, whose primary task is attaching and detaching the tow-rope as necessary.

Winch Recoveries. These can take various forms but usually involve moving an awkward object such as a log or a car body from one place to another and back again against the clock. Occasionally the participating vehicle has to be moved from the start to the finish of a section by using the winch. In addition to the driver, each vehicle usually carries two 'ground-crew' to operate the winch and set ground anchors. Additional equipment such as a pulley block may also be necessary. Any type of winch is suitable – drum, capstan, hydraulic or electric – and the event is designed to test the crew's knowledge, co-ordination and ability to pull through under very difficult circumstances.

The two recovery events and the point-to-point are true off-road competitions that no other vehicle can really enter, and as such they are good events to watch if you want to learn something. Sadly, all of them are becoming very rare now, although a few clubs have been trying to revive them in a slightly different form.

Hill Rally. I can't remember when I last heard about one of these events, so they must be getting very rare indeed! They are the exact equivalent of special stage rallies, with off-road stages to be attempted against the clock, and navigation exercises between them. The stage will be between a few hundred yards and a mile long, and may incorporate trials type sections. These events can include driving on public roads between sections.

Night Events. For some reason, a number of clubs like to make things doubly difficult by holding trials and competitive safaris at night. Not surprisingly, the judgment of rough terrain in the dark is very demanding, and you should not make a night event your first. Get some daylight experience before doing it in the dark!

Miscellaneous competitions

Many clubs like to promote the social and family side of their activities, and in addition to a weekend of off-road competitions, they may well organize something like a BMX bike trial for the youngsters, or a radio-controlled vehicle trial for the bigger kids. They can can also arrange caravanning on some competition sites, which helps to make the event a social occasion as well as a competitive one. The general friendliness of the off-road fraternity is almost legendary, and a club with a good social calender is not difficult to find.

6
Preparing for competition

by Bill Jones

Except for the very basic competitions such as gymkhanas and orienteering, all vehicles will be scrutineered before they are allowed to compete in organized events. This is done by the event officials, usually on the day of the competition, and it takes only a few minutes. The inspection is designed to confirm that the vehicle is safe, and that it complies with all the rules and regulations pertaining to the event in question. While preparing the vehicle for competition, you will have to ensure that it meets all the standards laid down by the RAC and your own club. It makes a lot of sense to contact the club's competitions secretary or chief scrutineer, who will gladly offer advice and help on any problems. Naturally different levels of competition require different standards of preparation, and even individual club rules can vary, so the information that follows can only be an overview of the main requirements of most RAC-affiliated clubs. The regulations are generally accumulative, which means that most of the requirements for the lower-level competitions are progressively incorporated into the more advanced levels.

fitted with seat belts, they must be used by both the driver and passenger. A navigator/co-driver may not compete with more than one driver in any single event, and there will be a minimum age (usually 14) for such passengers. The driver must hold a current driving licence and club membership card, and both should be available for inspection at all meetings. Smoking is not permitted by any member of the vehicle crew on any section.

All vehicles must be fitted with a positive method of closing the throttle in the event of linkage failure – this usually means an extra return spring fitted directly to the butterfly-spindle on the carburettor. The fuel tank must have a non-spill or leakproof cap with a self-sealing vent, and the battery must be securely fastened. Both the fuel tank and the battery must be kept separate from the crew compartment by bulkheads. There must be adequate towing points front and rear for recovery purposes. Apart from these specific points, the vehicle must be in a fit condition to pass an MoT test on the day of the event – which is not necessarily the same thing as having a current certificate!

Road Taxed Vehicle Trials

As the name suggests, all vehicles in these events have to be road legal, have a current Excise Licence (tax disc), and an MoT Test Certificate where applicable. Some form of rollover protection is required – a hard top, cab or tilt and frame – so totally open vehicles will not be allowed to enter unless they are fitted with a roll-bar or full roll-cage. Normal road tyres must be used, and penalties may be imposed at some clubs if the tyres fitted are considered too aggressive. Most clubs insist on a minimum tyre pressure for all events, and about 20 psi is common for RTV trials. If the vehicle is

Winch Recoveries

Because most vehicles entered in these events are roadgoing, everything in the previous section applies. All specialist equipment must be inspected by the scrutineer before the event commences, and it is recommended that protective clothing is worn at all times. All the equipment and crew must be on board the vehicle at the start and finish of the event. The clerk of the course has the power to stop any team if he considers that the method of recovery being used is dangerous to officials, competitors or spectators, or is damaging to the natural environment (trees, for instance, must be protected).

PREPARING FOR COMPETITION

Cross Country Vehicle Trials

Soft top vehicles are not permitted in these events – the minimum requirement is a manufacturer's hard top or cab, and preferably a roll-bar or full roll-cage. The crew must wear at least a lap strap while competing, but some clubs insist on normal seat belts or even a full harness. The All Wheel Drive Club expects trials vehicles to be equipped with a fire-extinguisher (minimum 2.5 kg BCF or BTM), and some clubs require an electrical cutout device which can isolate the battery in the event of a rollover. You will be expected to provide a substantial tow-rope for recovery purposes, and a one inch diameter (24 mm) nylon rope is advised. Most clubs do not insist on full safari specification for timed trials, but you will probably require a helmet to the correct standard.

Point-to-Point and Team Recoveries

In addition to everything mentioned in the previous section, drivers and crew for these two events will definitely need full harness seat belts and a helmet to the correct RAC MSA specification. Ask the competitions secretary of your club for the latest helmet specification, because these things can be changed occasionally and the same approved headgear is required whether you race karts or Formula One cars. Each helmet has to be 'stickered' by an RAC-appointed scrutineer. Your club should have details of the local man, and you will need to take the helmet to him for inspection; once he is satisfied that it meets the required standard, you will be given a sticker to confirm his approval. The vehicles used in these events must be fitted with a battery cutout. These are obtainable from all rally sport centres and some good car accessory shops for no more than the price of a few gallons of petrol. Peculiar to these two events is the requirement for a two-inch mesh metal grille to be fitted over the windscreen and behind the crew, for protection in the event of tow-rope failure. Because of the increasing difficulty of these events, all passenger/crewmen must be over 16 years of age.

Competitive Safaris and Hill Rallies

All the foregoing requirements still apply, but a roll-cage manufactured from specified materials and to a particular design must be fitted. If the vehicle weighs less than 1200 kg (2645 lb) and is fitted with a closed cab, some clubs will accept a substantial roll-bar instead of the full roll-cage. If no windscreen is fitted, a visor or goggles must be worn at all times. Rear marker lights and a horn must be fitted for all events, but adequately protected driving lights are obviously required for night events. Competition numbers must be fitted to the sides of the vehicle in a position that prevents them becoming obscured by mud, and they should be black on a white background. The numbers themselves will be issued to you by the competitions secretary of your club. An RAC Competition Licence is required to enter AWDC safari events.

A battery and ignition cutout switch mounted on the dash of an ex-Army Land Rover. These devices must be operable from inside or outside the vehicle. (All photos this chapter: Bill Jones)

General Advice

There are probably more retirements per competitive mile in off-road events than there are from any other branch of motor sport. This is mainly due to the incredible demands inflicted on both men and machine. Most problems will be simple mechanical breakdowns, but 'brain fade' (when the driver makes a major error of judgment) can cause just as much damage – if not more. During competitive safaris in particular, the vehicle's transmission, suspension, steering and chassis will be subjected to forces that are probably way above their design limits. It is therefore imperative that the vehicle is prepared as well as possible for each event. There is nothing more frustrating and time-consuming than travelling miles to an event, only to fail the scrutineering or retire on the first run.

Many drivers spend every spare minute between events working on their competition machines to bring them up to the highest possible standard. Reliability of the machine really is the name of the game, because being the fastest driver on the course is pointless if something silly goes wrong and you don't finish the event. Trials machines are also subjected to forces which can cause strange effects – such as carburettors cutting out at too steep an angle. Intermittent electrical faults can also worsen with this kind of abuse, and if the event is held on wet ground – or even crosses a pond or lake – the engine electrics will certainly need some preparation if you want to keep the ignition circuit dry. You might also need to pipe the air filter intake into a dry area (such as the cab) if you anticipate really bad conditions. Piping will also have to be applied to the axle breathers if you want to avoid sucking water into the axle casings.

Always carry plenty of spares (such as carburettor, distributor, hoses, half-shafts, wheels, wire, water and engine oil) when you enter competitive safaris – you will almost certainly need them! On the other hand, if you drive carefully in trials events you may never break a thing. Shock absorbers and springs need to be kept in good condition for off-road driving because they are tested almost

A dedicated pit crew and co-driver are useful assets when something goes wrong, and a good spares pack is essential. Here Robbo Aliperti replaces a half-shaft with some assistance.

PREPARING FOR COMPETITION

The lightweight 'tow chariot' has several advantages over a conventional trailer and takes up less room when stored.

beyond endurance. People go on forever about tyres – which are the best for which event, which give the best grip on a particular surface, which are the best all-round tyres and what is the optimum pressure for cross-country traction? Only trial and error will really tell you which tyres suit your vehicle and driving style, but the objective tests in Chapter seven of this book will provide some useful background information on the various makes.

Scrutineering on the day

Having entered the event by sending off your entry form and fee in advance, you turn up at the site. What happens next? Usually you would sign-in at the control vehicle or caravan, and collect a scrutineering card before presenting your vehicle for inspection. Some clubs scrutineer the vehicle first, but this is not common. At scrutineering your machine's brakes, steering, exhaust, cutout switch, seat belts etc., will be tested, and your helmet and fire-extinguisher checked. You may be asked to present your driving licence and club membership card either by control or by the scrutineer. You can fail the scrutineer's checks on something minor, which will mean going away to rectify the fault, or being warned to get it fixed before the next event. If you fail on a major problem that cannot be rectified on the site, you will not be allowed to take any further part in the event. So preparation is very important!

Always treat the scrutineer (and the other officials) with respect. They are doing a job which must be done to ensure that the high safety standards set in the past are continually maintained. There have been mercifully few serious accidents at off-road competitions and everyone wants to keep it that way. Despite the number of spectacular vehicle rollovers at safaris and CCVTs, it is unusual for anyone to sustain serious injuries. This is due entirely to the safety requirements laid down by the clubs and RAC MSA. Do obey all instructions given by the officials, and remember, a marshal's decision is always final.

57

The Drive

No amount of reading about competition technique will adequately prepare you for your first drive, but there are one or two things that you can do to make life slightly easier for yourself. My first piece of advice is particularly relevant to newcomers to the sport, but is also much practised by all good off-road drivers: try to watch other competitors on a section before you have a go yourself. I know that this is not always possible (you may be marshalled straight to the starting queue for instance, or the club might operate a rota for the start order and you get the short straw), but if you can get alongside the action for a few minutes, for goodness sake do so. You will generally learn an awful lot from experienced drivers: which gear might best suit the conditions, when to apply the throttle and when to back off, where to position the vehicle for a tight corner, etc. It also pays to marshal an event for the very same reason, and as a bonus you will gain a useful insight into how an event is run.

Remember that in trials events speed is totally unnecessary – you might never need to touch the throttle except for a steep climb, and the rest of the section can probably be done at tickover in the right gear. Sensitive control of the vehicle is critical, and you can help yourself achieve this by mounting a block of wood alongside the throttle pedal, so that your right foot can work very accurately over long periods without getting too tired. Also make sure that your throttle linkage is kept in tip-top condition, with no excessive slack or stiffness.

Always walk a trial section before driving it. You will be amazed at the number of experienced drivers who are still caught out because they failed to check the course – or even forgot which direction to go! When you are driving a section don't be distracted or embarrased by the banter from spectators: they are there to enjoy themselves and the more they (and the other drivers) can upset your concentration, the more likely they are to be entertained! A safari-type course might be too long for you to walk its entire length, but you can usually watch the competitors leave and then see them come back over the finishing line. Even that limited knowledge can be useful, because the condition of each returning vehicle (and its crew) will tell you a lot about the severity of the course. You need to be fit to drive one of these vehicles across open country, and very fit to do it at speed. If the course is rough, everyone will be exhausted at the end of the meeting.

A co-driver is not essential, either for trials or competitive safaris, but he can be very useful. While you are walking a trial section or watching other drivers for instance, your partner can be moving the vehicle up the queue towards the start. During the competition itself, he should be looking ahead to see which way the course twists and turns, while you watch every bump and hollow just a few feet in front of the vehicle and concentrate on driving. Where necessary, co-drivers can also operate the horn and windscreen wash/wipe system, and keep on eye on the mirror for faster vehicles coming up behind you. An extra pair of hands is also invaluable if any repairs need to be done on the vehicle during the event, because time lost here can lose you the whole competition.

Do take your time on the first run, especially in your first event: too many newcomers to the sport expect the vehicle to perform like a 4WD car in the RAC rally. It won't, and if you push it too hard you will end up breaking something expensive. This is years of hard-won experience talking now! Drive at a speed you feel comfortable with – that way you will stay in full control and might even make it to the finish. Your fuel costs will depend on your driving technique and your vehicle. In trials a couple of gallons would normally be sufficient for the day, but competitive safaris are another matter! These events are not exactly designed as economy runs, and I would suggest that any reasonable 4WD vehicle that achieves 6 mpg in competition is going a touch slow. To be competitive, 2–3 mpg is much more common.

Getting there

Buying a secondhand vehicle is a good way to get into off-road racing or trials events. The machine may well have seen better days, but it will certainly be fairly cheap compared with a new one, and will normally come ready prepared. After using it for a while, you will soon discover its weaknesses and be able to form a much clearer idea of what you want from a new vehicle. Remember too, that some of these secondhand machines are sold with a trailer thrown in – which is a very quick way of getting

PREPARING FOR COMPETITION

started. All the club and 'trade' magazines have advertisement sections which cater for everything from complete vehicle/trailer combinations to tyres and other useful spares.

Getting a non-road legal machine to and from events can be a major problem. Most competitors tow a trailer behind their 'everyday' 4WD, but both the trailer and the towing vehicle need to be fairly beefy to cope with the weight of a competition machine and all the necessary tools and spares. It can be hard work towing such a heavy trailer over long distances, and speed is naturally reduced, making some journeys a matter of days rather than hours. A rigid 'A-frame', which enables the towing vehicle to pull another without a second driver, is fine if the towed vehicle is taxed and tested and fitted with an overrun braking facility, but as most competition machines are not road legal, a trailer really becomes a necessity.

A very small minority of CCVT and competitive safari drivers have road legal machines which they drive to (and hopefully from) the various events. The preparation of these vehicles however, must be meticulous, and even then there is an obvious risk of sustaining damage during the event which will prevent you getting home. If there is an ideal solution it has to be the flatbed vehicle-transporter towing a caravan, or perhaps an American-style 'camper' mobile home towing the competition vehicle on a trailer. Expensively-converted coaches are used by some drivers, and these incorporate sleeping, cooking and workshop facilities – as well as holding the vehicle itself!

Flat-bed transporters are an ideal way of taking competition vehicles to events – if you can get your hands on one!

59

7
The rubber solution

This chapter is adapted from a report first published in Off Road and 4 Wheel Drive *magazine, and appears by kind permission of that publication.*

For anyone running an off-road 4WD vehicle a set of suitable tyres represents a major item of expenditure. Modern tyres tend to last quite a long time, which means you are stuck with any choice you make for at least a year, and probably much longer, depending on your annual mileage and the degree of abuse inflicted by your driving style.

Many factors need to be considered before you commit your hard-earned cash to any particular make of tyre. Such things as the weight of the vehicle, the availability of different rims, the top speed attainable, the proportion and type of off-road work you do, and even the predominant environmental conditions in which the tyres are to be used. There are also esoteric reasons for selecting a particular make. Some people still go for a tyre simply because they have always used them, as did their fathers before them. Some will always buy British, while some will always (or can only) choose the cheapest available. More often than not, the choice is limited to whatever the local tyre depot can supply from stock. Over and above all this however, is a powerful influence that most of us seek to deny, while anxiously searching for believable reasons to justify our choice of tyres. This is the *poseur* factor, which is one of the most potent weapons deployed by the marketing fraternity when they try to sell anything connected with cars: quite simply, the 'look' of a tyre has a definite persuasive value.

We have all got something of the *poseur* inside us, otherwise there wouldn't be so many 4WD vehicles swanning about. Most of these machines have an appeal that has nothing to do with owning vast tracts of untamed territory, towing caravans or boats (many ordinary cars are vastly superior for that), or the belief that our services are so indispensable that we must battle through to work on the three days a year when the roads are lightly covered in snow. There is an indefinable 'something' about joining the posh Land Rover brigade, and most of us simply want a piece of the action. Having decided on a 4WD vehicle to bolster our own self-image, the next stage is often to expand on the impression given by the vehicle itself. The choice of tyres is one of the most tangible ways of achieving this, because they give the clearest possible indication, to the layman at least, of the manly pursuits being enjoyed every weekend by the lucky driver.

Nearly everyone in the trade now seems to get a large number of enquiries about the suitability of various wheel and tyre combinations for particular vehicles. The choice is wide however, and sensible advice is virtually impossible to give without some kind of 'hands on' experience of the various makes now available. For this reason, *Off Road and 4 Wheel Drive* magazine set up a series of tests to provide a comparative assessment of the most popular tyres.

Strictly speaking, this sort of testing needs complete objectivity, with scientific measurements of coefficients of friction on different surfaces, cornering forces, tractive effort, rolling radii, heat absorption and all that sort of stuff – even a decibel count in some cases! Unfortunately there is nothing objective about off-road driving conditions, so any 'scientific' tests would be of very limited value. It was therefore decided to conduct the tests over the sort of terrain the tyres were designed for, and at the same time have as much fun as possible!

Eight sets of the most widely available tyres were obtained, with the stipulation that they should be mounted on appropriate wheels to legally fit a Land Rover Ninety Diesel Turbo. Each set of tyres was fitted in turn, and driven over the same cross-

THE RUBBER SOLUTION

country route in identical weather conditions. Two experienced drivers were used, both completing one circuit with each set of tyres before submitting a written report: there was no consultation between the drivers. The circuit itself included a wide variety of ground conditions and several miles of sealed roads.

Though somewhat subjective, it was felt that this was the fairest and most realistic way of going about the tests. Every effort was made to ensure that the ground conditions remained constant throughout the day, and by late afternoon everyone had a pretty clear idea of what each set of tyres was capable of. The findings of both drivers were remarkably consistent. Not surprisingly, the tread patterns that excelled in poor conditions displayed some disadvantages on the road, and vice versa, which just goes to prove what the manufacturers have been telling us all along – that compromise is the name of the game.

The look of a tyre still has a definite persuasive value.

Tyre-by-Tyre report

Armstrong Norseman: A good-looking American tyre with a mildly aggressive block tread pattern. It produces an acceptable ride with predictable handling, though locks-up relatively easily on damp surfaces. Noise levels are low.

Off-road it is a good all-rounder, but with no outstanding qualities. It's a well balanced compromise design, ideal for high tarmac road mileage but quite capable of off-road as well.

Avon Rangemaster: Clearly biased towards on-road use, this tyre nevertheless has a well spaced and

FOUR WHEEL DRIVING

defined tread pattern with relatively mild shoulder lugs to provide traction in off-road conditions too. On the road, the ride is excellent at speed though a trifle harsh when going slowly. All aspects of handling on the road are very good with high levels of grip, and there is no tyre whine.

Off-road, the ride is fairly firm with adequate grip in dry conditions. When the going gets damp or muddy though, traction is generally poor and directional control very limited. The tread soon clogs up and has difficulty clearing itself.

Dunlop SP Trak Grip Major: Primarily an on-road tyre with some off-road ability, but not much.

ABOVE
Pirelli MS26 being tested great on sealed surfaces, but for genuine off-road driving in the wet, it left much to be desired.

ABOVE RIGHT
The OR&4WD tests involved a lot of wheel changes for the two Land Rovers.

THE RUBBER SOLUTION

Excellent handling qualities on wet or dry surfaces with a firm ride and no noise. Impressive wet weather braking performance.

Off-road it was found wanting in any damp or wet conditions. Directional control was minimal, and it generally couldn't cope with off-road situations unless the going was firm and dry.

General Grabber MT: A fairly aggressive, block tread pattern with alternating sculpted shoulder lugs. On the road, its ride quality was good with predictable handling ability, but less ultimate grip than more conventional treads. Slightly noisy during cornering manoeuvres and producing a loud tyre whine on sealed surfaces at all times.

Off-road it proved to be extremely good in all conditions, giving very good directional control, and seemingly able to find traction anywhere. Its ability to climb out of ruts was better than average, though the vehicle was prone to grounding in a minor way due to the diameter being less than the 7.50s. The tread's self-cleaning efficiency was better than average, but it had trouble escaping the clutches of muddy ruts.

BF Goodrich Mud Terrain T/A: A fairly aggressive tread pattern with well spaced and prominent shoulder lugs. A slightly harsh ride on the road, but

There is nothing objective about such off-road conditions.

---

reasonable handling characteristics with predictable cornering and braking performance. The coarse tread blocks protested when cornered hard on dry tarmac, understeering earlier than a round-type tread.

Off-road, the smaller diameter caused noticeably more grounding. The ride was firm, and traction in all conditions was good with better than average directional control.

Michelin XCL: A purposeful looking tyre with a coarse block tread pattern, alternately extended on to each shoulder. On the road, ride quality is good, with good cornering and braking performance in dry conditions, but it can be unpredictable on damp roads. Mild tyre noise on sealed surfaces.

Off-road, traction was good in all conditions, particularly mud, giving excellent directional control. The ability to climb out of wet muddy ruts was limited however, despite the tread's good self-cleaning characteristics.

Mickey Thompson: Another good-looking tyre of American manufacture. Fairly aggressive, well spaced tread pattern, the theme of which is continued on to the side wall. On the road, the ride quality is good with cornering being entirely predictable right up to the high limits of adhesion. There is pronounced tyre noise on all sealed

THE RUBBER SOLUTION

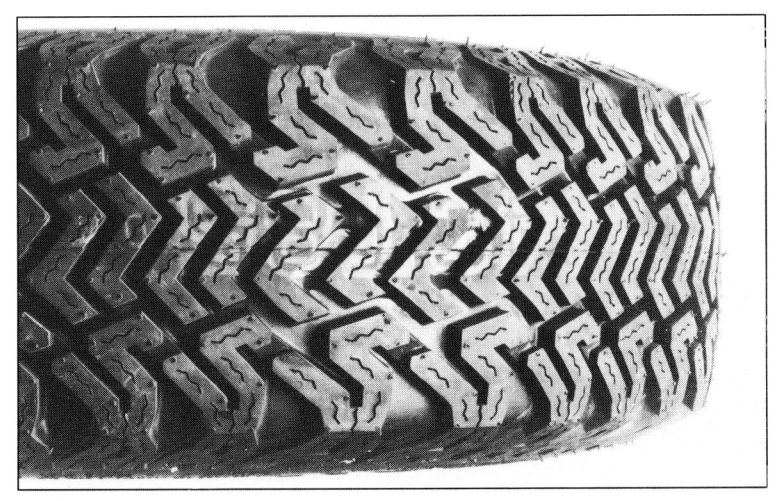

Armstrong Norseman.

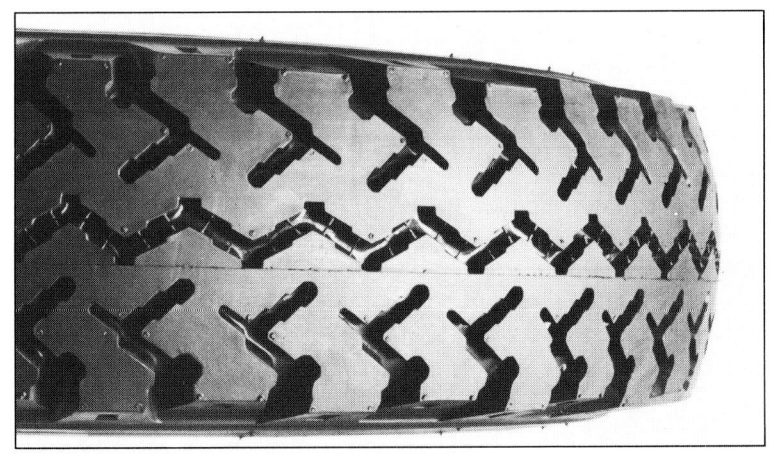

Avon Rangemaster.

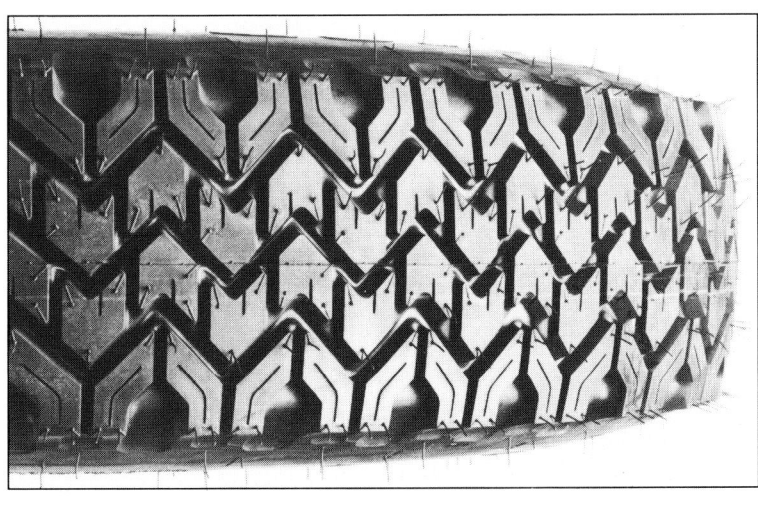

Dunlop SP Trak Grip Major.

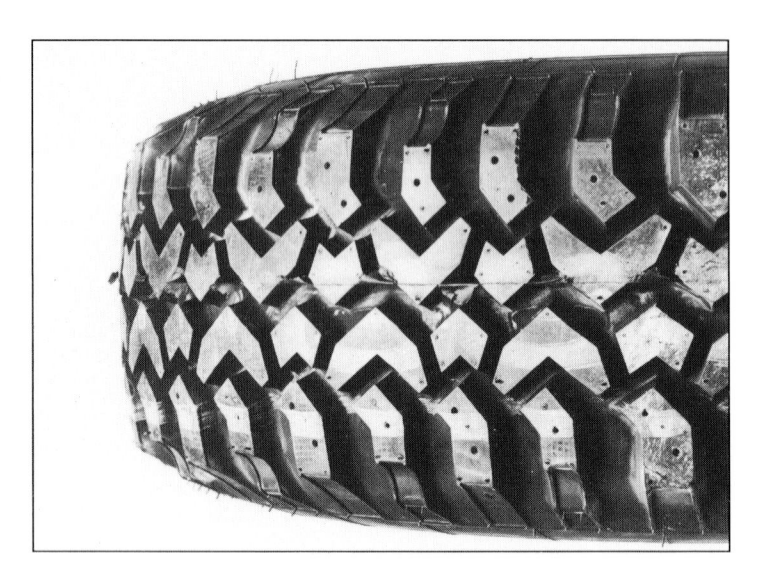

General Grabber MT.

surfaces. Under heavy braking on a dry road, slight weaving is induced, and on a damp surface the wheels will lock up and slide.

Off-road, traction was impressive in dry, firm conditions and on damp grass, but in heavy mud the tread tended to clog with a subsequent loss of traction. Spinning the wheels briefly cleared the worst of this, allowing a second bite, but this is not always possible. These tyres would clamber out of dry ruts with ease, but had difficulty in doing so in wet muddy conditions.

Pirelli MS26: Another on-road tyre, but marginally better off-road than others in the category. Handling and performance on sealed surfaces was excellent, wet or dry, but off-road it was a non-starter unless conditions were firm and relatively dry.

The final choice

These tests were primarily designed to provide an assessment of off-road tyres, consequently the bulk of the points to be scored were allocated to off-road performance, with a lesser number allocated to normal road characteristics. To a certain extent this distorts the findings, because most 4WD vehicles spend the majority of their lives on sealed roads, getting to and from the off-road bits. However, a glance at the comparative table quickly reveals that some tyres are better all-rounders than others, whilst some are clearly more cost-effective for vehicles that do a high annual road mileage.

Some enthusiasts will be prepared to sacrifice a bit of on-road comfort for the greater mud-plugging prowess of an aggressive tread, but others will be realistic enough to appreciate that the little real off-roading they do, does not justify specialist rubber. In this category one could consider the Avon Rangemaster, the Dunlop SP or the Pirelli MS26, all of which are splendid on-road tyres and more than adequate for most 'working' 4WDs when off-road.

The American tyres came out of the tests quite well, but being relatively wide had a definite 'feel' to them through the steering. None of them were obviously affected by road surface irregularities, but it is suggested that 9.50s are the largest tyres that should be considered for Land Rovers. Anything bigger requires a greater offset to the rim, and this can be detrimental to the wheel bearings. If you are not using the manufacturer's original wheels, do make sure that the ones you have are up to the job. The gross vehicle weights of the Land Rover Ninety and Range Rover can be nearly 2.5 tonnes, and a One Ten can weigh-in at something like 3 tonnes – so be careful.

Also ensure that the tyres themselves are up to the task. Your supplier should be able to advise you about these things, but if he can't (or won't) take your business to someone else. If you are using spoked steel wheels with flat centres, it is essential to check-tighten the wheel nuts after the first few

THE RUBBER SOLUTION

Goodrich Mud Terrain T/A.

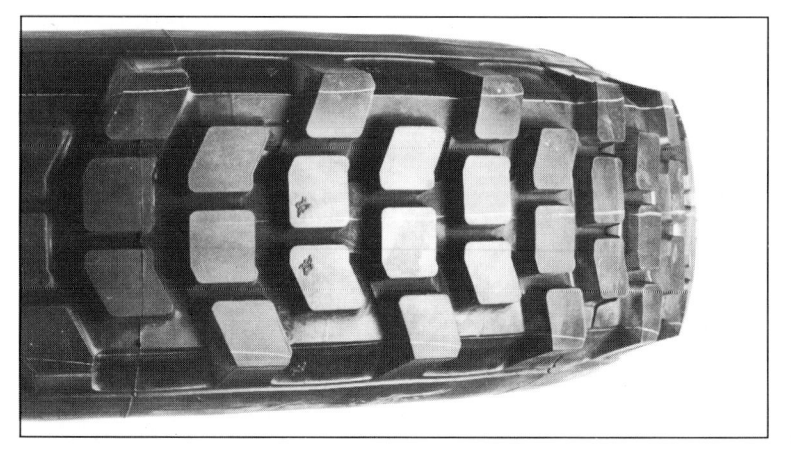

Michelin XCL.

Pirelli MS26.

FOUR WHEEL DRIVING

Always make sure that wheel nuts are correctly tightened, particularly when you use the spoked steel variety.

miles, and thereafter at regular intervals. Also be sure when fitting these wheels that no grit or other foreign body is trapped between the mating surfaces of the wheel itself and the hub. This is not such a problem with ordinary dished steel wheels, because the contact area is smaller, and the design of the wheel is such that correctly tightened nuts tend to self-lock.

Tyre pressures throughout the tests were set at 28 psi, but it is worth noting that a vast improvement in off-road performance can be achieved by lowering the pressures. This applies to all tyres, but care should be taken not to go too low – about 12 psi is the absolute minimum – otherwise you can unseat the bead from the rim with interesting results.

The object of these tests was not necessarily to recommend a particular make of tyre, but simply to assess them all in a logical way. Each set was awarded points (out of five) for various aspects of its on-road and off-road performance, and these were transferred to the accompanying table. Totalling the points in appropriate subsections will give you an indication of each tyre's competence in that role.

It can be readily seen that the Avon Rangemaster and Pirelli MS26 came out on top for an-road performance, closely followed by the Dunlop SP Trak Grip. In terms of pure off-road performance, the General Grabber was adjudged the best, followed in joint second place by Michelin's XCL and the Mickey Thompson Baja. Adding the two sub- totals together provides the best overall performers, but remember that the marking system had a deliberate bias towards off-road conditions. Bearing this in mind, the Mickey Thompson come out on top, with joint second place shared by the General Grabber and Michelin XCL.

Obviously every tyre on the list has its merits, and without considering price and availability in your area it would be quite impossible to recommend an individual best buy. At the time of the tests a number of suppliers were contacted in order to establish an average expected price for each tyre. It would be pointless to mention particular prices because inflation and regional differences will destroy their credibility in a matter of months, but listing the tyres in ascending price order might be helpful because their relative positions are unlikely to change very much. The cheapest tyre on the list was the Avon Rangemaster, followed by the Michelin XCL, General Grabber MT, Dunlop SP, B. F. Goodrich MT, Mickey Thompson, Pirelli MS26 and, at the top of the scale, the Armstrong Norseman. In some cases the average prices varied by only a few pence, so shop around if you want the best possible deal – and don't be afraid to haggle.

The General Grabber was considered the best off-road tyre.

THE RUBBER SOLUTION

8
When you get stuck

Even the most optimistic off-road driver will have to admit defeat one day and succumb to that unplanned pause in the progress of events known to all as getting bogged, or stuck. If you take your playtimes seriously, this situation is as inevitable as night following day, so you might as well know what you are up against.

You could come to grief on all kinds of surface, but mud is the most common and by far the muckiest to get out of. Sand is tricky stuff, and it can have a vice-like grip which often makes it the most difficult substance to escape from. Snow is no particular problem in itself, but it might conceal anything from sharp rocks to squidgy mud beneath its surface.

The first thing to understand about being bogged down is that excessive power cannot help. As a commonsense rule, all wheel rotation should stop as soon as forward motion is lost. It will do you no good at all to sit there with your wheels spinning furiously, because the agitation will simply dig you deeper into the trap and make it even more difficult to escape. Your expensive tyres could also be ruined – especially if one of them manages to find a buried rock that tears through the sidewall.

The best plan is to recognize quite early that you are stuck, and then apply some logical thought to the problem. A quick look under and around the vehicle will tell you whether you are going to be able to drive out of there, or whether you are in the spade trade. Before you start reaching for the shovel, try gently reversing and then going forwards again, and repeat the process as often as you sensibly can, in a sort of rocking motion. This may create a long enough rut for you to use as an escape ramp.

A few rocks, sacks or twigs thrown into the path of all four driven wheels can give that extra bit of traction to free the slightly stuck, but failing that, the big dig is on. If you have to dig, don't just peck timidly around the wheels, because this could make matters worse. The trick is to do things right the first time, so you only have to dig once.

Before you start, have a look round to make sure the way ahead is promising, because nothing is more pointless than to free yourself from one big hole only to plunge straight into another one. When you are sure you know which way to go, get the jacket off and have a good dig until you are confident that you can get away in one determined movement. Take it easy on the way out and drive a good bit clear before stopping, then go back and fill in your excavations. The last point is important because you may have to return along the same route, and it would be really silly to fall into a hole of your own making!

Jack and Winch

If you really cannot dig your way out – and this is quite likely – a different plan of action is called for. Any jack that will raise the vehicle a foot or more, will provide enough clearance to enable you to put brushwood or stones, etc, under the wheels to provide that little bit of extra traction. The hi-lift jack is an ideal instrument for the purpose: this fearsome device can be used to elevate the vehicle to a fair old height, so you can decide whether to lay a brushwood carpet, or to take a more extreme course and deliberately push the vehicle off the jack and over to one side – hopefully onto firmer ground. A big base plate or plank must be used as a support, unless you want the weight of the vehicle to push the jack into the ground as soon as any pressure is applied.

The built-in winch is often favoured for recovering a bogged-down vehicle, but even these have their problems. Most of them are fitted immediately behind the front bumper, which is fine if you want to go forwards, but a retreating extraction is a bit more difficult. Passing the wire underneath a well bogged-down vehicle is almost impossible at the best of times, but even if you do manage it, the chances are still high that it will snag on something important as soon as the load is applied. Pulling vital bits off the underside seems like a high price to pay for a 'simple' recovery operation.

Another fairly common problem with winches is that the wire always seems to be at least 10 ft short of the nearest anchorage point. This is called sod's law. If you are afflicted by this malevolent spirit, or if you are stuck on an open moor with the nearest tree at least 30 miles away, you will need to revert to the 'plan-B' arrangement of using ground anchors to pull you clear. These are available in a variety of forms, ranging from purpose-designed tools to the old trick of burying the spare wheel. Using the spare wheel sounds a bit daft, but it can easily take the load of unsticking a bogged-down vehicle without any kind of distortion. All you need to do is attach the winch cable securely to the steel centre, bury the whole wheel vertically until the top is just level with the ground, and operate the winch in the normal way. When the vehicle is free, remember to recover the wheel and fill in the trench. The local farmer will not be too pleased if one of his sheep falls into a hole left by a thoughtless off-road driver!

Tow-rope

No 4WD vehicle should ever venture off the road without a good tow-rope. These are available in man-made or natural fibre, and in a wide range of manufactured forms. Natural fibre ropes are generally preferred for off-road use because they are much stronger than the man-made variety, and they absorb the shock loads of releasing a bogged-down vehicle without too much stretching. The maximum length permitted on the highway is 15 ft, but this is not really long enough for recovery purposes. You need a long rope to enable the towing vehicle to get a reasonable run before it snatches the stuck vehicle out of its hole. A 30 ft length with a loop and shackle at each end (together with a spare shackle) should be adequate for off-road use, but it will have to be doubled-up for any normal road towing.

When you secure a tow-rope to either vehicle, make sure that the attachment points are major load-bearing parts of the structure. The pulling forces involved can be phenomenal, and if the structural integrity of these points is compromised in any way, they can be torn away from the vehicle as soon as the rope takes the strain.

Snatch rope

Many off-roaders are now great devotees of the kinetic-energy recovery rope, or snatch rope. These are like oversized pieces of elastic that stretch, storing kinetic energy all the time, as the towing vehicle accelerates away. When the rope reaches its stretch limits, it imparts a shock load to the stuck vehicle, and then tries to contract to its normal size again. In doing this, it adds its own stored energy to the pull of the towing vehicle, and imparts a terrific thrust to the stationary load.

Without any doubt the scientific principle is sound, and snatch ropes are most effective – but they can be absolutely lethal unless both vehicles are structurally perfect. There was an incident at an off-road meeting in southern England some years ago when a bogged competitor was 'rescued' by a geriatric vehicle using a powerful snatch rope. When the rope reached its stretch limits, the shock load tore the rust-weakened tow ball and its associated bracketry away from the accelerating towing vehicle, and the kinetic energy stored in the rope recoiled the whole assembly backwards, firing it through the stationary vehicle's cab. It smashed through the windscreen, sliced off the passenger seat headrest, and carried on to punch its way out through the back window. Luckily the passenger had vacated the vehicle just before the recovery operation began, but if she had still been in the seat she would certainly have been killed.

You either love these ropes or you hate them. I know that I personally would never recover anyone, nor allow anyone to recover me using one, and the British Army (who seem to know a thing or two about recovery operations) will not allow them to be used on anything other than armoured vehicles. You must decide for yourself whether you wish to use one. They certainly work, but the energy stored in them can be released with almost explosive power, and this could have potentially lethal results. If you are in any doubt, don't use them.

Obviously all off-road drivers try to ensure that

FOUR WHEEL DRIVING

they never get stuck, but most of us are realistic enough to know that it does happen. In theory of course, if you use the proper rules of anticipation and take care with your angles of approach, you should never put yourself in that situation in the first place. A 'tactical withdrawal' is always preferrable to getting your vehicle well and truly bogged. That being said, the time will inevitably come when enthusiasm triumphs over common sense, and recovery is the only answer. When this happens to you, always remember to take the utmost care with towing or winching, and keep the area around all the vehicles free of non-essential people. If anything breaks, it is far better to have a dented body panel or two than a severely injured bystander. Recoveries are no different to any other aspect of off-road activity, if you stay sensible you stay safe.

ABOVE

At this point you should start thinking about climbing the bank on the other side. Can you do it? Never be ashamed of making a 'tactical withdrawal' if you have any doubts.

ABOVE RIGHT

Obviously a case of enthusiasm getting the better of wisdom. A bogged vehicle is a familiar problem to off-roaders, and a recovery crew is quickly on the scene. But reversing is not recommended because the low reverse gear ratio of the recovery vehicle will not match that of the forward gear of the escapee. Here they're having trouble with the last few feet.

RIGHT

A second attempt, going forward. The crew are standing well clear.

WHEN YOU GET STUCK

9
Every winch way

This chapter is adapted from a report first published in Off Road and 4 Wheel Drive magazine, *and appears by kind permission of that publication.*

When it come to off-roading, the ability to use a winch successfully should be second only to your ability to drive. Indeed, good winching technique may save you from situations that your driving has dropped you in! That's obviously a little unfair because anyone who has done any form of even mildly serious off-roading will know that a winch is often the only way through.

Although winching is certainly very useful, it can also be great fun – but there are elements of potential danger to the uninformed practitioner. What then, are the techniques needed for safe, foolproof winch operation? There's certainly no great mystique about it, despite what some people may imply. Anyone can become a good winch operator, and that's not something you can necessarily say when it comes to driving. Follow some basic rules, use common sense, always be aware of the potential dangers, pick up some tips from the experts and you should be able to get out of most sticky situations.

To learn more about practical winching, Nigel Fryatt and John Beese from *Off Road and 4 Wheel Drive* magazine, went to Eastnor Castle to consult the expert Land Rover team led by Roger Craythorne. Two Land Rovers were used for the cross-country exercise; a Ninety Turbo Diesel and a V8 petrol-engined One Ten. There were also two different winches; an 8000 lb Warn 8274 (probably the winch factory-fitted to more Land Rovers in the last ten years than any other), and the much more recent Fairey Husky (from FW Winches) with a potential pulling power of 8500 lb.

This chapter is concerned with the practical aspects of winch operation, not with the efficacy of any of the products used. Suffice to say here that there are an impressive number of winches and accessories on the market, and it always pays to shop around. Seek advice from colleagues or experienced club members before you spend what could turn out to be a large amount of money on a fully-equipped rig. We would advise strongly that you think hard before you go for a winch with a pulling power of 10-12,000 lb. These are really commerical and industrial winches. For recovery of a single 4WD vehicle, or pulling a boat out of the water, 8000 lb is more than enough. After buying the winch itself, you will need some protective clothing and a few standard accessories – similar to the equipment used during our day at Eastnor.

It is possible to recover a vehicle without any assistance, but we would advise against it. People who drive across rough country for a living are often alone and therefore have no choice, but if you use a 4WD vehicle for pleasure, always try to take someone with you whenever you go off-road. Ideally you should travel in company with another vehicle (this should be a golden rule if you have no winch), but if you insist on going solo, an adaptable partner, a good winch and the right sort of accessories should see you through.

Successful winching really needs two people – the winch operator and the assistant – and you should agree in advance who will do what, and stick to it. Confusion of the two roles can lead to important safety precautions being unconsciously ignored.

The Operator's Tale

As the title suggests, the operator is in charge of actually using the winch via the remote hand-

EVERY WINCH WAY

ABOVE
The Land Rover demonstration team probably know more about winching techniques and equipment than most of us will ever know.

LEFT
The Warn 8274 winch will be familiar to most Land Rover enthusiasts.

FOUR WHEEL DRIVING

The 8000 lb Ox Winch (Superwinch) – seen here on a Series IIA Land Rover – is just one of a wide variety of these machines now available. (Phot: *I.C.M. 4 × 4 Equipment*)

control unit. Always unwind the electrical cable to the control box before connecting it to the winch, and check it carefully for any fraying or breaks in the casing. There will be a good 6 ft or so of this cable, so if you are not careful it could easily get tangled around something – possibly even the wheels. Once the connector is plugged in, wind the cable around the driver's door mirror and lay the control unit on the bonnet, or pass it through the open cab window and leave it on top of the fascia. Never have the control in your hand while anyone's fingers are near the winch. Your assistant should always want to see where the control is before he, or she, gets useful fingers anywhere near the wire on the drum.

You must decide on the anchoring point you are going to use before you get all the equipment out of the vehicle. Ideally you want a solid anchorage positioned directly ahead of the winch. This is obviously not always possible, but a small offset is no particular problem. If a straight-line anchorage is not immediately available, you can always ease the situation by using ropes and snatch blocks. A good solid tree is the most likely anchor, but always check to make sure that it has leaves or buds on it – even quite thick trees can be pulled down by an 8000 lb winch if they are dead. If a fully grown tree is not available a group of small trees or saplings can be 'roped-in' to share the load. All trees used in this way must be protected from damage.

Once you have decided where the winch will be secured, check the route and proposed angle of the pulling wire. If it looks as though the wire will touch the ground under strain, make sure there are no sharp rocks or protrusions that could damage it. If necessary, find a log to act as a fulcrum, or dig a small trench for the wire to run through.

Now is the time to go back to the winch and unwind the wire. There are two ways of doing this; easy and hard. The easy way is to use the winch motor, but if you do this just bear in mind the effect it will have on the vehicle's battery. If you are a solo vehicle and you flatten the battery, you could be in big trouble. If you know that you are going to do a lot of winching, always use the drum's free-wheel facility and physically pull the wire out. This is not a difficult job at all really – especially for the operator, because it's the assistant's job! If you find that the winch's clutch is reluctant to disengage when operating the free-wheel, a short flick on the hand control will move the wire slightly and should be enough to jerk it free. As the assistant is paying out the line, the operator should examine its condition as it comes off the drum.

While the assistant is securing his end of the line to the anchorage point, the operator must maintain tension on whatever wire remains on the drum. This can be done by hand (using very strong gloves, preferably heavy-duty leather) or by holding it firmly under a boot. If the wire on the drum is allowed to go slack, it will no longer wind neatly when you start to winch, and that could be disastrous: you would certainly ruin a very expensive wire, and the winch could jam if all the incoming line tried to wind itself around one small section of the drum. If you are paying out all the line, keep at least four turns on the drum to ensure adequate grip.

The operator now waits for the assistant to indicate that everything is secure at his end. It is at this point that you should start using your own pre-arranged sign language. With the engine running and the possibility that you are many yards apart, shouted instructions are of little use.

Agree the code between you beforehand. One popular signal is for the assistant to take 'biting' movements between the fingers and thumb of one hand, each bite indicating a single blip on the operator's hand control. A rapid succession of biting movements tells the operator to keep his finger on the button. You will also need to know when the assistant wants you to pay out the line or pull it in, and most importantly, when he wants you to stop.

Take up the slack, stop and check that everything is safe and secure. The wire should be winding nicely onto the drum; if you are using snatch blocks ensure there are no twists in the wire; and check that all the anchorage points are holding. You are now ready to start winching.

At this point the operator is bound to discover that he's on the wrong side of the wire for some reason – life's like that! The shortest route to where you want to be is always just a quick step over the wire. DON'T, whatever you do, try it. It may seem like a real pain to walk all round the vehicle – especially in thick mud – but it's nothing to the pain you would feel if the taught wire suddenly snapped or came adrift.

The operator's position during winching is always safer than the assistant's: he will be inside the vehicle if he intends to winch and drive at the same time, or at the very least walking alongside the vehicle during a winch-only recovery. In both cases he is protected to some degree from the whiplash effect of a broken wire.

The hand control unit of a Fairey Husky winch. This enables you to drive the winch from the cab, and keeps the operator well away from the danger area should the wire break.

Actually winching a vehicle is very satisfying. The power of one of these little machines is awesome as you watch it extricate a stricken Land Rover from some bottomless bog. With control box in hand, you can just leave the winch to do all the hard work, while you keep an eye on the drum to make sure the wire is winding properly. Once again, however, battery life is very important, and you may find that the winch needs a little help. If this happens, the operator will have to get behind the wheel and use the hand controller while driving.

Winching and driving does take a little practise. The idea is to drive when you have grip and winch when you don't. The important thing to remember is that the vehicle's clutch must be either in or out –

FOUR WHEEL DRIVING

no half measures, and no deliberate slipping. Not only will this help save the clutch, but you will also find out much sooner when you have the grip to continue driving. You will need teamwork to do this effectively, with the assistant alongside watching the driving wheels and shouting instructions through the open passenger door window.

After a successful recovery, feeding the wire back onto the drum needs considerable care. The wire must be kept under tension to ensure that it feeds on firmly and evenly, but this can be dangerous towards the end of the operation. Every operator must be fully familiar with his or her winch, and in particular know how much wire will be gathered in during the motor's brief overrun. When you only have a short length of wire remaining, which must be kept under tension and then secured, carelessness here could lead to lost fingers.

If you know you will be needing the winch again soon, particularly if you could be in water or buried

ABOVE LEFT
A good solid anchorage point is needed – preferably directly ahead of the winch.

ABOVE
A decent sized log will lift the wire clear of any ground obstruction and prevent damage.

ABOVE RIGHT
Holding the wire under a boot will keep it taut while the winch assistant is securing the anchorage.

RIGHT
If the wire is not winding evenly onto the drum, stop and re-wind before you put the whole rig under tension.

EVERY WINCH WAY

in deep mud, it might pay to keep a length of the wire free and attached temporarily to the driver's door mirror. If the winch then gets submerged in goo, at least you can find the wire without too much trouble.

Always take care of the wire. Clean it after use, and make sure there are no flattened sections that could indicate areas of weakness. If the wire frays at any point it should be replaced. Do not take the risk of using a damaged wire.

The Assistant's Tale

Organization and anticipation are probably the most important attributes needed by the assistant. He is responsible for looking after the equipment and helping to make decisions about the best technique for winching a vehicle out of trouble. The job is not a difficult one, unless you choose to ignore the basic rules – in which case it becomes dangerous.

We soon learned that wearing suitable clothing can make winching safer and easier. The sort of terrain that can stop a V8-powered Land Rover is probably hazardous even on foot. A sturdy, well-fitting pair of boots is important, and if there's a lot of water around, some form of wader will often prove useful. It's important that the assistant doesn't over-dress, because he needs to be able to

FOUR WHEEL DRIVING

work hard without overheating or being restricted by his clothing. He needs to look after a variety of pulleys, shackles, chains, and so on, while keeping his hands free, so large pockets are a definite advantage. Ropes and tree slings can be tied around the torso where they will be easily available, but they can restrict access to jacket pockets. Large side trouser pockets are possibly the best solution.

It's really up to the individual to work out the best system for organizing the equipment. Before driving into the wilderness it is helpful if everyone involved knows where all the tackle is stowed. If equipment is simply hurled in the back of the vehicle with rope and chain doing the octopus hug, you are heading for problems. Each piece of kit should have its place.

Drawing out and feeding in the wire is potentially hazardous for the assistant, and it is important that he knows the safest method, and has an effective means of communication with the operator. The assistant must check that the operator is well away from the hand control unit before he puts his fingers anywhere near the winch. If this is done, there is no danger of the operator accidentally winching when the assistant's hands are vulnerable. The operator should always place the control unit on the fascia of the vehicle, or on the bonnet, where it is clearly visible. To preserve the battery charge, the wire should be pulled out with the winch in free-wheel mode. It is well worth familiarizing yourself with engaging and disengaging the drive if you are new to the particular winch, as each system requires a slightly different technique. When handling the wire protective gloves must be worn. A splinter from a fraying metal wire can cause a deep and painful wound.

The assistant needs to instruct the operator when to pay out and draw in the wire. Hand signals are essential because vocal instructions cannot compete with engine noise and the distances involved. A popular form of signal, and one we found successful, is for the assistant to point away from the vehicle when he needs the wire paying out, and to point at the vehicle when he needs it drawn in. The amount of wire needed either way can be indicated by making beak-like impressions with the other hand, opening and closing the thumb and fingers in an exaggerated fashion. Each 'bite' should signal an individual blip on the hand control. All these procedures seem awkward at first, but after you get used to them they make the job a lot easier.

Never step over a fully tensioned wire. It may look inviting, but if it breaks it will ruin more than your day!

ABOVE RIGHT
Winching and driving needs close teamwork.

Before the assistant starts pulling out the wire, he should be certain of the eventual anchorage point. The ideal anchor is in direct line with the winch, so that the wire traces the route the operator is hoping to drive along. If the winch is made to pull at an angle, the efficiency of the system is reduced. It is useful to remember that the initial gearing of any winch is lower when virtually all the wire has been payed out because the effective diameter of the drum has been reduced. It is therefore better to start a difficult recovery with as little wire on the drum as possible. However, at least four turns should be retained at all times to keep a good grip on the spool. The wire should be kept taut on the drum to avoid it recoiling and tangling. Winding a loose or tangled wire is dangerous, and at the very least will seriously damage the equipment.

With the winch spool on free-wheel and the assistant trekking off into the wilderness pulling out the wire, the operator should leave the cosy confines of the driver's seat and place the hand control on the bonnet of the vehicle, where it is easily accessible. Wearing the appropriate gloves, he can then help the assistant pull out the wire and indicate to him how much remains on the spool. When paying out or guiding in the wire, it should be passed hand over hand and not slipped through the gloves. While the operator is maintaining the tension, the assistant can attach the wire to a suitable anchorage point. For most of our recovery experiments at Eastnor Castle the wire was attached to trees using a sling. This consists of a broad band of woven nylon ending in two loops, which was sleeved in a nylon jacket to enable the loops to be drawn together relatively easily when the sling is placed around the trunk of a tree. The wire must *never* be wrapped around a tree and hooked to itself. This will certainly damage the tree, possibly damage the wire, and halve the strength of the rig. The tree must be healthy and stout enough to take the strain. Trees

FOUR WHEEL DRIVING

that might be too weak individually can be linked together for strength. The sling must be attached as near to the base of the tree as possible. If you do not own a sling, use a good stout rope as a substitute, but it must be wrapped round the trunk several times to protect the bark. When coupling up any part of the winching rig, you must make sure that there are no kinks, knots or twists in any of the equipment, as these will form weak points under strain. If the ground has ridges or obstructions that might cause damage, the wire can be protected by allowing it to slide over a log at the critical point.

Once the assistant is happy with the rig, he should return to the vehicle and take over tension-keeping

ABOVE LEFT
Pre-arranged hand signals are a vital safety precaution when using a powerful winch.

ABOVE
A good tree sling should be long enough to enable several small trees to share the load.

RIGHT
Snatch blocks are swivelled around the wire...

FAR RIGHT
... and then attached to the tree sling with the aid of a bolted coupling.

from the operator. The slack wire can now be fed slowly back onto the drum, with the operator using the hand control and the assistant taking care to keep his hands at least five feet away from the jaws of the winch. When all the wire is under strain, care must be taken to ensure that no one steps over it in case something breaks. If any part of the rig seems at all likely to give way, it would be wise to place a blanket or coat over the mid-point of the taut wire: should the rig then snap, it will only recoil as far as the obstruction.

If the operator is to winch and drive simultaneously (to ease the load on the battery), the assistant will need to check that the wire is feeding onto the drum correctly, and keep an eye on the wheels to see how much grip they are finding. The operator should always try to keep the wire under tension, and verbal instructions from the assistant will help to achieve this by telling him when to winch and when to drive.

Once it becomes clear that the vehicle can make progress under its own traction, the assistant instructs the operator to stop. After applying the handbrake, the operator then winds out a few inches of wire to make sure that the vehicle can hold its position. If it starts to slide backwards, the team can either resume winching to find a better spot, or secure the vehicle by tying it to a tree with a separate rope, and re-positioning the winch rig to gain more ground. In some cases when the operator is winch-driving and the vehicle begins to gain traction he will not want to stop. In this case the assistant must be ready to grab the wire well forward of the vehicle to maintain tension on the spool and prevent the loose wire from being run over. Clearly this can be a hazardous exercise on slippery ground, and personal safety should never take second place to a few yards of extra progress.

The operator helps to recover the wire by taking up the slack while the assistant disengages the tackle. The assistant then feeds the wire evenly onto the spool while signalling to the operator when to work the hand control. The winch hook must not be left to hang down below the vehicle where it might snag, but clipped neatly into one of the towing eyes mounted under the bumper.

Many 4WD enthusiasts fit a winch to their vehicle without really knowing how to use it. There is a lot

FOUR WHEEL DRIVING

In wooded country the back end of the winching vehicle can be tied to a tree for added support.

to learn, and after a day's intensive tuition from the experts it was obvious that we had improved a great deal – but only on the basics. If you have never been winching before it is advisable to learn the technique from an experienced off-roader. And the only way to really improve your technique is to practise as much as you can.

The accessories

It is essential that all your winching equipment is in good condition and suitable for the job. Check the manufacturers' guarantees, and be careful to match breaking strains with the pulling power of your winch. Apart from the winches and tree slings already mentioned, the basic equipment we used included two staple-spun polypropylene ropes (one long and one short), two snatch blocks, a choker chain and two couplings. We also used some excellent vehicle ground anchors from Land Rover's own accessory range. Roger Craythorne particularly recommended the staple-spun ropes as being very strong with enough stretchability to take the strain of a modest snatch-type recovery. The different lengths of rope increased the options.

The snatch blocks consist of a pulley wheel mounted in a swivel casing that allows the block to be attached to any part of the extended winching wire. The casing swivels together around the wire and forms an eye which is used (often with the aid of couplings) to join the snatch block to the rig – all much easier to understand when you have the equipment in your hands. The blocks can be used as pulleys to increase the mechanical advantage of the winch. For example, to halve the load on the winch, the wire is run out to the anchorage point, where it is run round the pulley wheel in the snatch block, before being returned and attached to the vehicle. If an even lower gearing was needed, a second snatch block could then be attached to the vehicle, and the wire run round this and back to the anchorage, thus increasing the mechanical advantage threefold. The limits to this are the numbers of snatch blocks you have, the length of your wire and the strength of your chassis.

Another common use for the snatch block is to improve the angle of winching. If the only suitable anchorage point is at too acute an angle to allow efficient winching, or if there is an obstacle in the line of approach, a snatch block can be attached to the extended wire and then linked, via a separate rope, to a second anchoring point. This makes an angle in the pulling wire, effectively allowing you to winch round corners. We used either the choker chain or one of the spare ropes to provide this link, but always taking care to protect the tree.

If there are no natural anchorage points available, you will have to find an effective ground anchor – particularly if the bogged-in vehicle is the one without a winch. In these circumstances, any attempt to pull it clear with nothing more than a stationary recovery vehicle might well result in the safe vehicle being pulled into the mire by the stranded one. Proprietary ground anchors are available from a variety of sources, but they are not cheap for the weekend man and are more often used commercially. The big advantage of the manufactured items is their convenience and ease of use. With Land Rover's version, all you need do is drive the recovery vehicle onto the anchors and let its weight embed them firmly into the ground. To recover the anchors, you simply hook some chains over the bumper and reverse for a few feet. They are effective, but rather bulky for the weekend off-roader to have permanently aboard his vehicle. In wooded country a ground anchor is rarely necessary because the back end of the winching vehicle can be secured to a tree with a tow-rope, or the front bumper can be wedged up against a tree.

If you are on your own, completely treeless and without a proprietary ground anchor, the alternative is to bury the spare wheel with the winch wire attached to it. This is obviously hard work, but it seems to do the trick (See Chapter 8).

The winch wire should always be neatly wound and fully secured before moving off.

10
Accessories for 4WD

This chapter is based on an article that originally appeared in Land Rover Owner *magazine, and has been used by kind permission of the author, H. Torosyan of Bearmach (London) Ltd. (All photographs kindly supplied by Bearmac or Land Rover Parts and Equipment Ltd.).*

Very few vehicles lend themselves to customization quite as well as a modern 4WD. The market for these versatile machines has greatly expanded over the last decade, and accessory manufacturers are now falling over themselves to provide everything an owner could ever need – either catering for his special interests (shooting, fishing, boating, etc) or simply to provide the vehicle with a touch of individuality.

With so many accessories around, it is sometimes difficult to know what does, or does not, represent good value, especially if you just want to enhance the appearance of a vehicle without necessarily changing its function or versatility. For special-interest groups the choices are more clear cut, because the function of a gun-rack say, or a dog guard, is far more likely to influence its design and use of materials than any thoughts of aesthetic appeal.

One thing that is clear, is the need to place special emphasis on the quality of any accessories you may choose. The last thing any of us want is a vehicle that looks as though it came from a weld-and-bend workshop, with bits of gas-pipe and wire mesh all over the place. Good quality accessories will not greatly add to the value of your vehicle, but they will certainly make it easier to sell. Even if you intend to keep the machine for some years, you will still want to ensure that the accessories do not deteriorate more quickly than the vehicle itself. The initial quality of anything you buy is obviously a major factor in maintaining its appearance.

Before you rush out and buy the first thing you see, shop around and consider as many alternative makes as you can. Check the various 4WD magazines for reputable manufacturers of the item you need, get hold of loads of brochures, and ideally go along to a dealer and see the chosen accessory on a vehicle. Ask questions about the materials used in its manufacture, the gauge, the weight and whether the coating materials are durable for the sort of driving you do. Any good dealer will have all the answers at his fingertips, but if yours does not, alarm bells should sound.

Every accessory you buy ought to be intelligently designed and incorporate a sensible fixing system. Most people are reluctant to drill big holes all over the body panels of an expensive vehicle, so award a few extra points to designers who have recognized that fact and used brackets that pick up on existing bolts or screw holes. Also be aware that an aluminium-bodied vehicle might suffer more damage in an accident than would otherwise be the case, if its fixed accessories are poorly designed or badly mounted.

Nudge bar

One of the most familiar accessories for an off-road vehicle, these large protective frames have their origins in the occasional need for professional off-road drivers to push directly against a static load – another vehicle perhaps, or a fallen tree – but they are more often used now to enhance the illusion of a 'country-gentleman's carriage' or a safari-type adventure vehicle.

Four-wheel drive vehicles can be extensively customized.

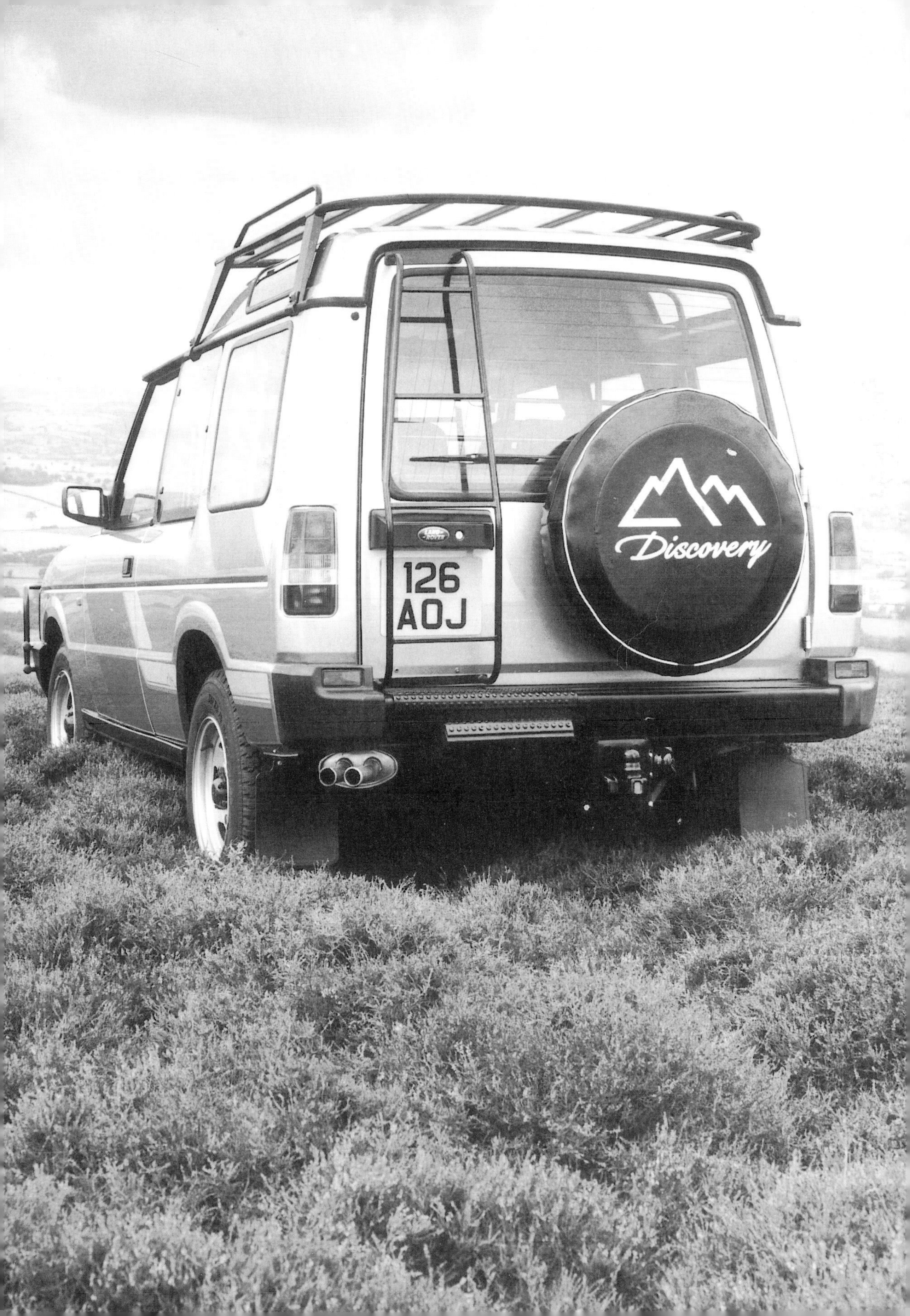
126
AOJ
Discovery

FOUR WHEEL DRIVING

Dog guards are now available for most vehicles . . .

. . . but few manufacturers provide a fully waterproof liner to save the upholstery from soggy dog syndrome.

ACCESSORIES FOR 4WD

Gun clips are a real country-gentleman's accessory, but the carrying of guns in this way is now illegal in the UK.

Extra lights can be mounted in the centre of most nudge bars.

Wraparound nudge bars can increase the overall width of a vehicle.

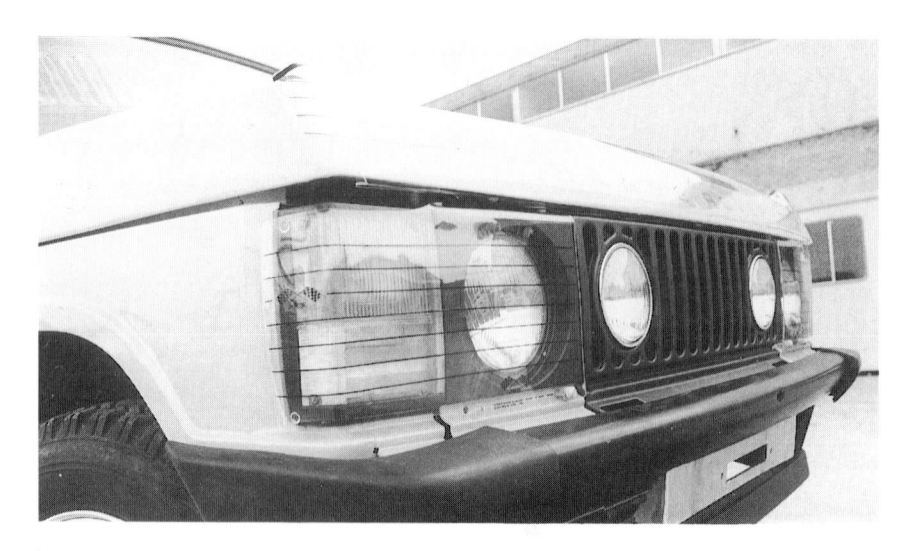

FOUR WHEEL DRIVING

TOP
Plastic lamp (and bonnet) guards do an excellent job, but somehow look out of place on an expensive vehicle.

ABOVE
Metal slatted guards certainly look better than plastic shields, but offer less actual protection.

A nudge bar will only afford protection against very minor traffic accidents, but it can be helpful during slow-speed manoeuvring or for parking mishaps. There are several different designs, with either straight or wraparound bars, and most of them can carry optional lamp mounts, top rails or centre plates, For city traffic the wraparound versions are generally favoured, but they can increase the width of the vehicle slightly and you need to take more care when reversing. The top rail is useful because it enables you to judge the bonnet length more accurately, and for off-road use it can also protect the bonnet from overhanging shrubs or branches.

ACCESSORIES FOR 4WD

ABOVE LEFT
Hinged lamp guards allow easy access for maintenance or cleaning.

ABOVE
If a steel lamp guard is mounted on an aluminium body, both the lamp and the guard may survive a minor traffic accident, but the softer vehicle body could suffer damage. Choose your guards carefully.

A centre plate is helpful for both city and off-road driving because it protects the vehicle's grille and any auxiliary lighting that may already be fitted. On some designs, additional lights can actually be mounted on the centre plate. A good wraparound bar should offer protection to the sidelight and flasher units.

You must be sure that the design you choose does not obstruct any of the vehicle lights, including the flashers. Also make certain that the bonnet can be opened easily, and that some provision has been made to allow you to change or adjust the headlamp units without removing the bars. With Land Rovers this is not so much of a problem, but on Range

FOUR WHEEL DRIVING

TOP AND ABOVE
Lamp conversion kits can change the appearance of a vehicle with the minimum of trouble.

ABOVE
A quad conversion achieves the most radical changes by equipping the vehicle with matched square headlights and spotlights.

ACCESSORIES FOR 4WD

Rovers the gap behind the bars tends to be smaller, so hinged lamp guards are a useful feature.

The actual appearance of a nudge bar is largely a matter of personal choice, but do ensure that the one you choose does not exceed the width of the vehicle by too great a margin. Make sure that the surface finish and welding are neat, and that there are no spatter marks or sharp edges. Nylon, as opposed to 'ordinary' plastic/polythene is the most durable finish. It is normally harder, chip-resistant and almost impervious to ultra-violet (sunlight) degradation, and if localized damage does occur Nylon will not peel – unlike most other coatings. Epoxy painted or polyester powder coatings are not as good as Nylon, and will certainly chip or peel

LEFT
If you fit 'designer wheels' remember to buy a set of locking devices, or you may wake up one morning to find your chariot resting on a pile of bricks.

BELOW
Winches are expensive machines, but they are almost indispensable for a hard-working off-road vehicle.

FOUR WHEEL DRIVING

with the slightest stone damage. Nylon coatings are more expensive than other finishes, but the extra protection is well worth the difference.

In most cases the nudge bar mountings simply pick up off the front chassis member, utilizing the same bolts as the bumper. Fitment is therefore a simple matter of slackening off the bumper bolts, offering up the bar and then re-tightening. On some of the older Land Rovers, or on models biased towards the utility market, the nudge bars bolt directly onto the front bumper.

Lamp protectors

A lot of 4WD owners fit external lamp protectors, which are particularly useful for off-road conditions where whiplash and stone damage can be a con-

Tow-bars are particularly useful devices, but watch your off-road departure angle!

RIGHT
A fold-down rear step can make access to the vehicle much easier.

tinual problem. Inevitably a small amount of light is lost with these devices, but in most cases this is kept to a minimum by good design. Fitting auxiliary lights can always compensate for any losses if necessary.

It is obviously impossible to totally protect driving lights, but the two kinds of guard that are most commonly available do a good job and are well worth the investment. The so-called Perspex lamp shields are actually made from a modern acrylic plastic; they are simple, cheap and afford the best possible protection with minimum loss of light. They will need to be removed occasionally and washed in warm soapy water, but apart from that there are no maintenance problems. Very small scratches can sometimes be removed with light abrasives (such as toothpaste or jewellers' polish), but anything deeper will necessitate replacement.

Metal slatted lamp guards are not as light-efficient as the plastic shields, and small stones can penetrate the slats. They do, however, have the advantage that matching rear-lamp guards are available, and if you buy the hinged version they make access to the lights very easy.

The slatted guards are well suited to on-road vehicles because their appearance is generally more pleasing and maintenance is easier: some makes even have matching centre grille sections. The small amount of light lost with these units is of no real consequence. The plastic shields look out of place on a high quality vehicle, but they are more efficient all round – particularly for off-road use. Whichever type you choose, make sure that they can be easily removed or hinged out of the way to allow access for cleaning, maintenance or adjustment. If you want hinged guards, check the appropriate vehicle construction and use regulations because some countries do not allow them.

Most of these guards need holes drilled in the bodywork to locate and fix them, and this could cause problems with an aluminium vehicle. Vibration and the weight of a steel guard might cause the drilled aluminium to wear, which could result in the fixings coming loose. Also, if the guard itself was too strong, a minor traffic accident could cause excessive damage to the body panel – damage that would not have occurred had the lamp guard been made of more crushable aluminium. Remember that these guards should be treated as sacrificial devices, designed to absorb a minor impact before any damage is done to the more expensive parts of the vehicle.

There are many different manufacturers of slatted guards, so shop around before you choose one. If your vehicle has an aluminium body, buy aluminium guards. Inspect the fittings supplied, to ensure that the screws and washers are all plated, and if the kit includes any brackets, check that they are nylon coated. If you choose the acrylic shields, again look for plated fixings, and check to see how easily they can be removed for cleaning. All front guards should require a minimum of drilling, and the main fixtures should be concealed under the bonnet to prevent theft. Some rear slatted guards can be fitted by slackening off the inner light casing and sliding in a clamping plate. This use of existing screws is ideal because it avoids the need for further drilling.

Lighting Conversion

A number of lighting conversion kits are available for Range Rovers. These not only enhance the overall light output of the vehicle, but also add a certain distinction to the front-end appearance. Most of these kits are supplied complete with all the necessary relays and wiring, and are certainly the easiest way of installing auxiliary lights. Some of the kits can be used to update and re-style earlier models, but make sure that the one you choose is really compatible with the vehicle because there are problems with some air-conditioning and oil-cooler systems. The most radical change can be achieved by removing the original grille and headlamps and replacing them with a quad conversion kit, which equips the vehicle with a pair of square headlamps and matching spotlights.

11
Four-wheel drive expeditions

This chapter was prepared by K & J Slavin (Quest) Ltd, expeditions consultants to Land Rover Ltd.

The number of expeditions undertaken by 4WD vehicles increases every year, and the success or failure of each one is clearly linked to the thoroughness of its pre-departure preparation and planning. The more information you can gather beforehand on the route and all its associated problems, the better your chances of achieving the goals of the expedition on time and within budget. The vehicles involved must also be prepared to the highest possible standard, and the team must be capable of looking after them at all times with the minimum of assistance. This chapter is primarily concerned with Land Rover expeditions, but many of the observations will equally apply to other 4WD vehicles.

There are sound arguments for and against both petrol and diesel-engined vehicles, but you will have to make a choice based on your knowledge of the route conditions. A petrol engine has a greater power and torque output, and the maximum speed of the vehicle is generally higher. New petrol-engined Land Rovers are cheaper to buy than their diesel equivalents, and the fuel is cleaner and less pungent to transport: petrol engines are also quieter and mechanically much more straightforward to service and maintain. On the other hand, petrol is much more dangerous in terms of fire risk, which could become a significant factor if any leakage should occur or if there is any risk of the vehicle toppling over in really rough terrain.

Diesel fuel is generally cheaper to buy, and the fuel consumption of diesel engines is significantly better than that of petrol. This will give you a big increase in unrefuelled range, which could be handy in sparsely populated areas of the world. The low-speed torque of a diesel engine provides much better pulling power in conditions such as soft sand, and because it has no electrical ignition system, the diesel is more suitable for 'wading' or driving in flooded regions. Although the engine and fuel system are more difficult to work on (never run completely out of fuel in a diesel!), you should get up to 40,000 miles from the unit before you run into any mechanical problems.

Loading

There is a tendency to take too much equipment on a long expedition, with the obvious danger of overloading the vehicle. Recommended axle loadings should always be taken seriously because they were calculated to provide for your long-term safety – a vital talisman when you are 500 miles away from the nearest settlement. If anything breaks due to overloading you will only have yourself to blame. A lighter vehicle is always faster and more economical, and it will certainly last longer.

Towing a trailer in cross-country conditions is a hazardous operation, and should be avoided if at all possible. If you cannot manage without one, make sure it is fitted with wheels that are as large as possible to reduce rolling resistance. If the wheels are exactly the same as those on the vehicle, so much the better, because in cases of dire emergency the trailer can then provide spares for the vehicle.

Roof racks should generally be used for carrying lightweight, bulky items, and the load should be evenly distributed. Remember that the normal maximum loading for a Land Rover roof is only 150 lb – and that includes the rack itself! If you need to carry more, the Land Rover 109 Series III station wagon can be modified to take a heavy-duty rack. This involves strengthening the bulkhead and windscreen, and fitting internal tie-bars across the floor and below the ceiling to keep the vehicle fairly rigid: external reinforcing bars can also be fitted if

FOUR-WHEEL DRIVE EXPEDITIONS

ABOVE
Roof racks are a practical means of carrying jerrycans or fairly light, bulky equipment, but if you want to carry heavier loads you will need to strengthen the vehicle bulkhead, reinforce the windscreen frame and fit internal tie bars.

LEFT
The 1-tonne Land Rover 101 is one of the best vehicles ever produced by the Solihull factory; now becoming much more widely available as used examples are released by the MOD.

FOUR WHEEL DRIVING

When production of the Land Rover 101 was terminated, the 127 emerged as its natural successor. The double crew cab and high capacity pick-up body provided ample load space and a reasonable level of passenger comfort.

necessary. Jerrycans can be carried on the roof in a specially constructed lockable compartment at the rear of the rack, but travelling with full cans should be kept to an absolute minimum unless fuel is unavailable locally. Plastic and metal jerrycans, both new and secondhand, are available from most military-surplus or camping stores – but beware of leaks in the used cans. Cheaper Hungarian or Czechoslovakian jerrycans are also becoming available in Britain. For extra stowage inside a station wagon the rear bench seats can be removed and a plastic mesh partition fixed behind the second row of seats: this will allow baggage and equipment to be packed right up to the roof without any risk of it being thrown forward under braking.

The right Vehicle

For a two-man expedition the hard-top Land Rover is usually the most suitable vehicle, but for more people (up to five) you will need a station wagon. Windows can be fitted in the side panels of a plain hard-top, but if you intend to bring the vehicle back into the UK the modification will make it liable for a new band of Excise Duty. If you intend to leave the UK permanently, check with your local Customs and Excise Office because you should be able to reclaim the extra tax.

Canvas topped pick-up vehicles are not the obvious choice for long expeditions, but they can be ideal for project work overseas. If you have to deliver one of these to its eventual workplace, you will need to be extra vigilant about security during the long overland journey, because your cargo will obviously be far more vulnerable than it would be under a hard-top. No matter what vehicle you drive, it can easily fall prey to pilfering, so you will need to stay alert and not leave it unattended unless it is securely locked or in a guarded compound. Never leave tempting goodies on show, even when the vehicle is locked up; and if you get out of the vehicle in an inhabited area, close all the windows and lock the doors or your precious things will disappear in an instant. Sensible packing and overall security on a journey of this nature are very important, and because standard door locks are one of the first things to fail, you should fit a sliding, lockable bolt to the inside of the rear door.

When you are preparing for a long expedition a new vehicle would obviously be ideal, but this is not always affordable. If you use a secondhand one (and lots of people do), find out as much as you can about its history because your life could depend on it for several months. Have it thoroughly overhauled and serviced by a reliable mechanic, and don't start penny-pinching on such a major check – if something needs fixing, get it fixed before departure, or it could fail when you are out in the wilderness. Always check that the engine and chassis numbers conform with the vehicle's papers, because any discrepancies here will cause constant delays at

Now is not the time to decide you really shouldn't have ignored the recommended axle loadings, and should have checked out that mysterious oil leak. A well-prepared expedition should allow the participants to really enjoy their environment without being distracted by too many unforeseen problems. Life should certainly be interesting, but a safari-style holiday should never be all blood, sweat and tears.

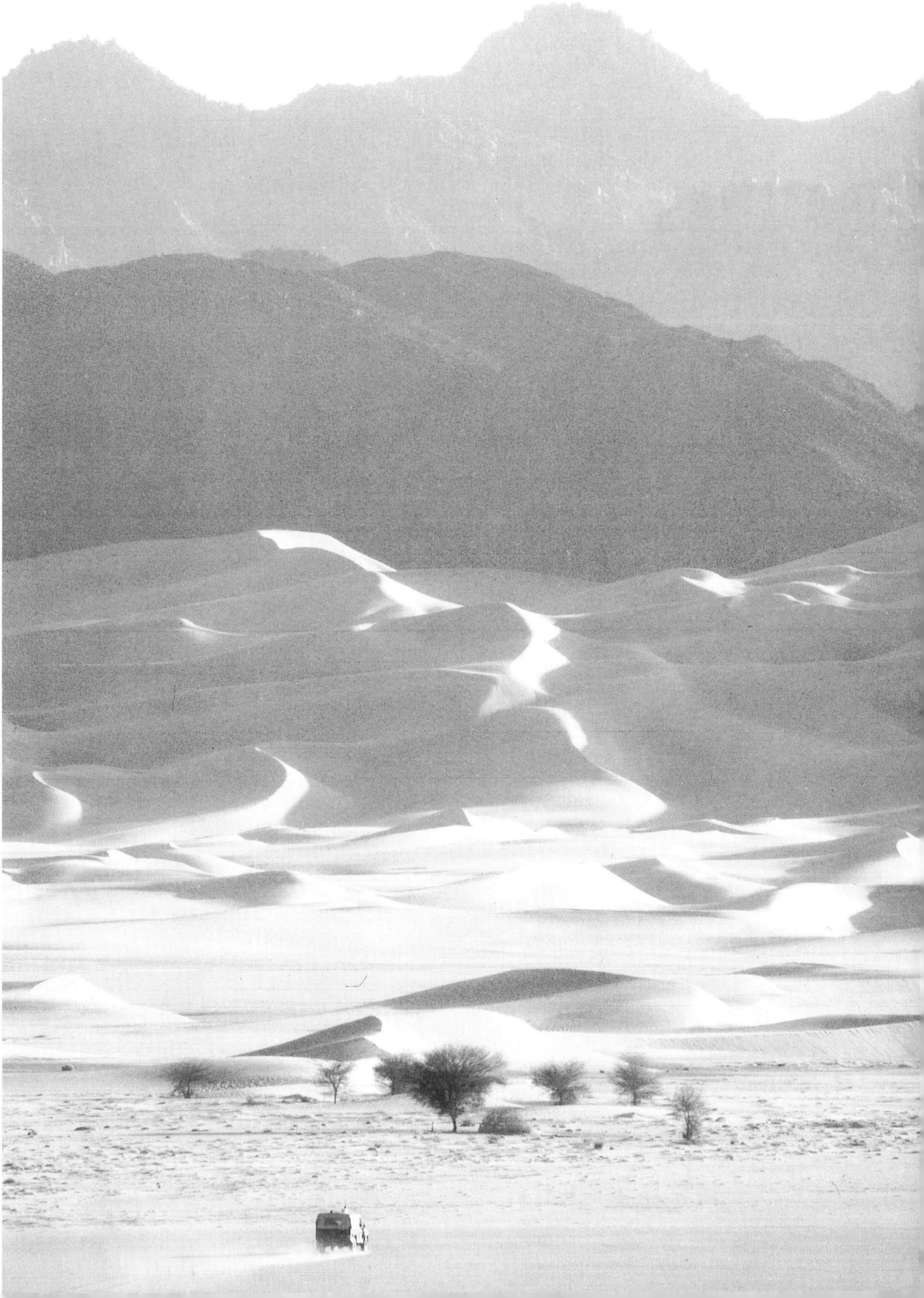

border posts, and could result in confiscation of the vehicle and a term of imprisonment for you!

Pay particular attention to suspension and engine performance. In the course of time faulty suspension will react badly to off-road terrain, causing possible structural and mechanical damage to other parts of the vehicle. Reduced engine performance and poor compression will certainly make the vehicle sluggish and tiring to drive, and increase your fuel consumption significantly. If the engine is not in reasonable condition to start with, the extra strain of a long expedition could lead on to far more serious problems. Tell-tale oil leaks should be examined and rectified, and any loose nuts or fixings should be tightened at the earliest opportunity and then checked regularly throughout the journey. All drivers involved should have enough mechanical ability to carry out routine maintenance, servicing and repairs – in adverse conditions if necessary. A vehicle handbook and workshop manual are essential, and you should also take as comprehensive a spares and tool kit as your funds will allow. Always work within reasonable weight limits, especially with tools and spares.

Documentation

A *Carnet de Passage* is vital. This document is like a passport for the vehicle and in certain countries it has to be stamped on entry and exit. It can be an expensive element of your expedition budget because a bond may have to be deposited with a bank to satisfy the requirements of the AA and RAC, who will actually issue the *Carnet*. You can also obtain the *Carnet* through an insurance company which will put up the bond for you, but in this case your money is not refundable when you return. Some people still think they can drive off into the wilderness and sell their vehicle wherever they end up, but this is wrong. If you want to do this, the ground has to be well prepared beforehand, and the *Carnet* must be stamped in confirmation of the intended sale. If you fail to make these arrangements before departure, you stand to lose the total value of your deposited bond.

Tyres

Tyres are an important consideration for such a long trip, and you should base your selection on the kind of terrain you will be crossing and the distances involved. Well-organized expeditions are expensive enough, but tyres are central to the success of the whole venture and your choice should not be limited by budgetary constraints. Chapter seven of this book will give you a good general idea of what to look for and a comparative analysis of some of the most popular makes. In addition to the tyres mentioned in that report, expedition experience has shown that the Michelin XS is ideal for continuous and extensive sand driving, and the same company's XZY is a good 12-ply which has very durable sidewalls and is suitable for more varied terrain. It is advisable to take two spare wheels with you if you anticipate a great deal of off-road driving, together with several additional inner-tubes. It would also pay to visit your local tyre depot before departure, to ask their advice about 'in-the-field' puncture repair techniques: a practical demonstration would be helpful, and if you can do the job yourself a few times, so much the better.

The best jack to carry with you (weight permitting) is a 36- or 48-inch Hi-Lift. This will allow you to change wheels with ease, and if you get stuck in deep sand it will also allow you to raise the vehicle high enough to get sand ladders under the wheels. For desert expeditions, four short sections of sand tracking – or two longer sections – can be a great time and energy saver. Never go anywhere without shovels!

Some common-sense advice

The success of an expedition depends almost entirely on the performance of your transport, so cross-country vehicle handling and general driving expertise are crucially important. An overland journey to India or Alaska is nothing like a day trip to Blackpool, and any inexperienced off-road drivers must practise manoeuvring the vehicle in difficult conditions before leaving home base. The importance of gaining this experience and confidence cannot be emphasized too strongly.

Remember that speed should never be the objective of a serious expedition: rushing headlong towards your destination can cause unnecessary vehicle damage which will jeopardize the whole trip. Make sure you are comfortable in the vehicle and well supported by the driving seat, or long stretches of off-road driving will wreak havoc in

Although winches are expensive machines, they are indispensable on any expedition worthy of the name – especially for self-recovery. This Warn unit is popular with Land rover users.

your back muscles. In soft sand or boggy conditions, reducing the tyre pressures will increase their contact area with the ground, improving traction and minimizing the tendency to sink – but you must remember to bring them back up to normal pressures once you are free of those conditions. If the going begins to look at all dubious, stop the vehicle, get out and conduct a reconnaissance on foot. Before crossing a difficult section you should select a suitable gear ratio and stick with it until you get to the other side. Bear in mind the action of differentials on a 4WD vehicle and choose a path where the conditions under both wheels of the same axle are similar: this also applies to finding the correct angle of approach to an obstacle so that you avoid lifting a wheel off the ground. Always be careful to maintain ground clearance under the chassis, and ensure that the approach and departure angles of any slope are within the vehicle's limits. Avoid deep wheel ruts, sudden changes of slope, and obstacles such as rocks which could interfere with the chassis or differentials.

When in doubt about a particularly difficult section, get all the passengers out of the vehicle and ask them to guide you through. Having them outside will improve the vehicle's ground clearance slightly, and they can watch the underbody as it passes over particularly nasty obstructions. For descending a steep slope, select the lowest possible gear ratio and allow the engine to provide its full braking effect. Using wheel brakes on a big slope can induce sliding and loss of control. Always apply the accelerator pedal cautiously because sudden power surges can easily cause wheelspin on a loose surface. For a vehicle travelling solo, a good winch can be a great asset for self recovery – but remember to take a tow-rope with you, and get some experience of using the winch before you set off.

A daily maintenance routine, no matter how difficult the circumstances, is most important. Try to formulate a sensible check-list before you depart, and then make sure that time is allowed during the daylight hours of every driving day to carry out the necessary inspections. Never take the vehicle for granted. Stay alert for any unfamiliar noises from the engine, transmission and suspension, and investigate each one as quickly as possible. Remember that continuous loud music will prevent you hearing the first signs of distress from your vehicle.

Long expeditions can be great fun, and if you prepare yourself thoroughly they can be completed with the minimum of fuss and bother. If, however, you skimp on the planning and ignore sensible advice, you can quickly make yourself look really silly and perhaps even put your life in danger. Basically it will be your resourcefulness and strength of character that will pull you through the difficult times, but if you manage to overcome all the problems and complete the project, you will have had the experience of a lifetime.

12
Camel Trophy

The last great adventure

The Camel Trophy expedition must be the ultimate in off-road driving adventure. In these days of air-conditioned comfort and jet travel it seems almost inconceivable that anyone would willingly undertake a surface journey across 1000 miles of the roughest terrain on earth. But undertake it they do, and people from all walks of life now apply in their hundreds of thousands to take part in the event.

The whole idea originated during 1980, in what was then West Germany. Organized and financed by R. J. Reynolds – the makers of Camel cigarettes – the event was conceived as a test of individual driving skills and wilderness technique, and it was important that no team should gain unfair advantage over another by having a more powerful or better equipped vehicle. To make the event as 'pure' a test of human endurance as possible, all the teams were given identical equipment, a proposed route, and as much support as they needed to ensure their collective safety. The support teams were not assigned to individual vehicles or crews, but acted in the best interest of all the competitors.

The first expedition was a major achievement, but it was really just a miniature version of the Camel Trophy as we know it today. Three teams, all of them from Germany, used AMC Jeeps to drive for 1000 miles along the Transamazonica Highway in Brazil, spending a total of 12 days battling their way through the mud and heat of the Amazon Jungle. There were no Special Tasks to complete as there are today. The whole event was so successful that a second expedition was announced shortly after the teams arrived back in Germany.

During 1981 the event was held in Sumatra, the largest of the Indonesian chain of islands, set in the steamy heat of the Indian Ocean. Although it was still open only to German drivers, there was an avalanche of applications for the ten team places that were made available, and the British Range Rover was selected as the only vehicle likely to be tough enough to withstand a gruelling drive through 1000 miles of deep equatorial jungle.

The sponsoring company is a very large, multinational organization, and after the publicity attracted by the second event, its marketing people in several other countries began to sit up and take notice. What had started as a purely German initiative, became an international competition in 1982 when two teams each from Holland, Italy and the United States joined the expedition – each sponsored by the publicity budget from their individual countries. This has now become an established pattern, with each Reynolds division organizing its own pre-event publicity and team-selection trials, and paying the costs of its own 'local' team. Standards are set centrally so that everyone is working to the same formula.

The 1982 expedition was held in Papua New Guinea, and Special Tasks were introduced for the first time to make judgement of the overall winner a little more objective. During the two previous events, a winner of the Camel Trophy itself had 'emerged' from a process of observation by the support team. This system of marking recognized that an arduous expedition through uncharted territory is a totally co-operative exercise, with everyone helping each other through the difficult

---

ABOVE RIGHT
If this exercise at the Camel Trophy selection trials looks a little hazardous for the driver and the Discovery, that's because it is.

RIGHT
Unloading a One-ten from a floating pontoon.

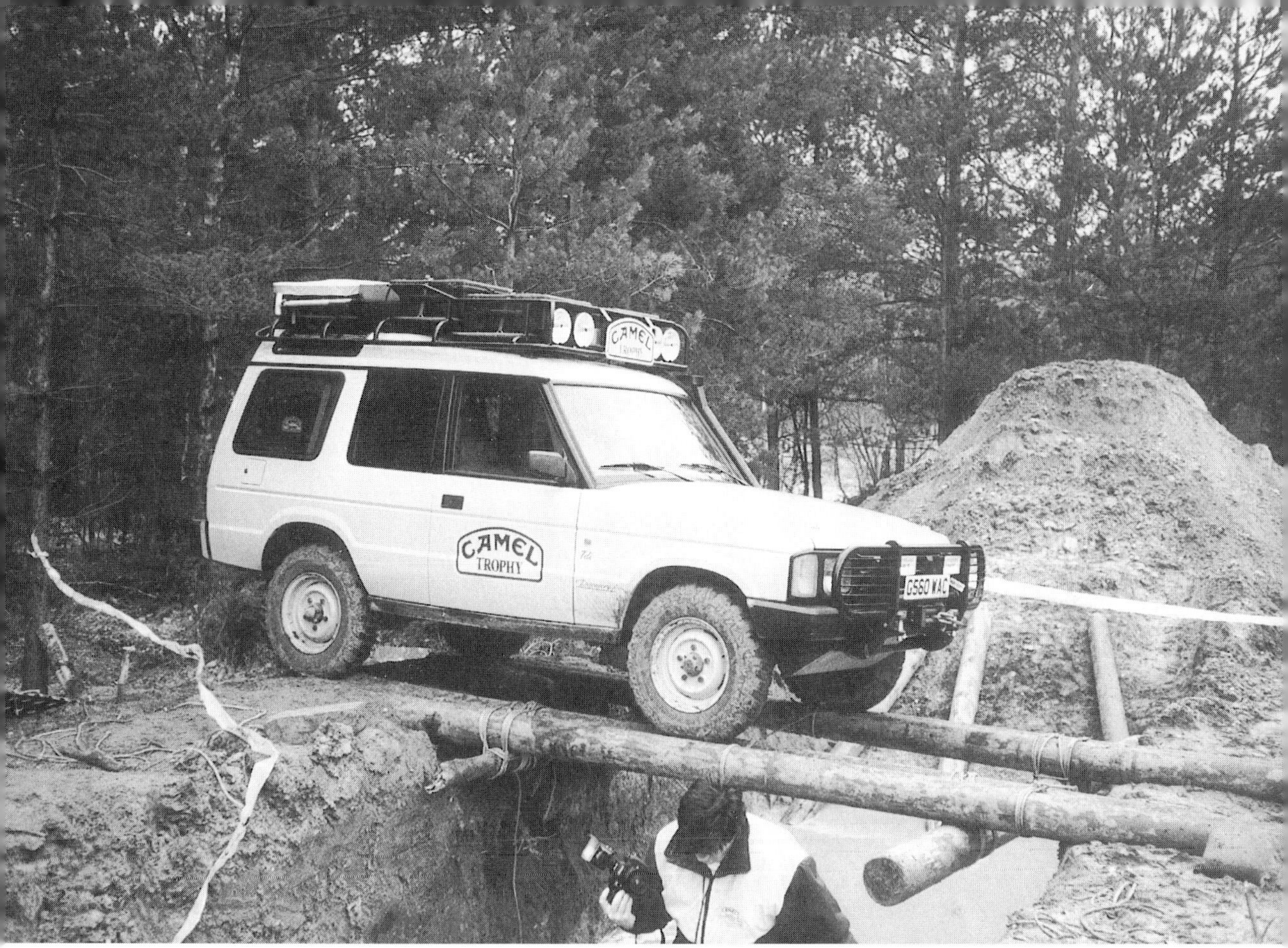
CAMEL
TROPHY
G560 WAC

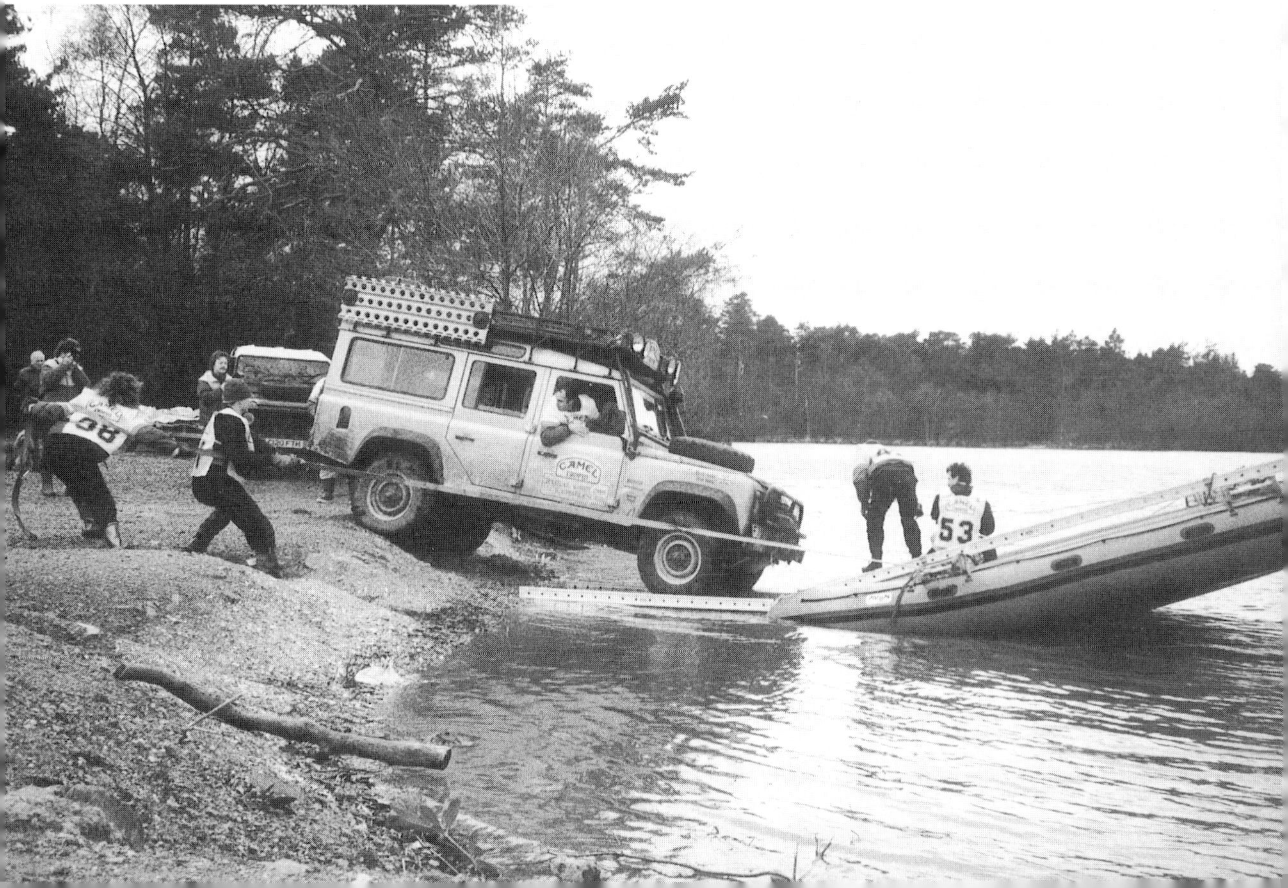
CAMEL
TROPHY
38
53

FOUR WHEEL DRIVING

CAMEL TROPHY

LEFT
Crocodile file, Siberia 1990; 16 national teams took part.

ABOVE
36 Land Rovers line up prior to shipping to Dar es Salaam for the '91 Camel Trophy.

sections. The trophy was therefore given to the team that made the best *overall* contribution to the success of the venture. This was very difficult to decide on an even-handed basis: someone with a morale-boosting cheerfulness in great adversity is often just as important to the long-term well-being of the group as a brilliant technical achiever. The Special Tasks are now undertaken equally by every team, and their relative performances can be judged without any dispute.

The first international event was won by the Italians, but the progress had been painfully slow and many a night was spent building bridges to get the Range Rovers across fast-flowing rivers. This was not a problem faced by the teams in 1983, because the route then consisted of a 1000 mile meandering 'track' between Kinshasa and Kisangani in Zaire – the first time the expedition had visited the African continent. Some of the temperatures during the trek north reached a searing 45 degrees centrigade and humidity hovered around the 95 per cent mark, making conditions in a vehicle cab almost unbearable. The terrain varied from

FOUR WHEEL DRIVING

The drama and endeavour of the 1990 Camel Trophy in Siberia: swollen rivers, quagmires, bears, armed horsemen, scorching days and freezing nights. The UK team of Andrew Dacey and Richard Tomlinson took third place behind the Dutch and the victorious West Germans.

CAMEL TROPHY

knee-deep mud to arid desert sand, with the occasional rock-strewn gully or shale escarpment thrown in for good measure. Despite the severity of the course everyone seemed to survive quite well, but the Dutch team did more than enough to take the trophy home with them.

To mark the fifth anniversary of the event, the organizers decided to return to South America and continue along the Transamazonica Highway – effectively starting the 1984 expedition where the first one left off. The rainy season, however, had reduced the planned route to an area of deep floods, so it had to be abandoned. The alternative trail was not much better, but at least it was passable. The 12 two-man teams persevered through heavy rain and deep mud, but had to stop three times to build bridges before their Land Rovers could cross the swollen rivers. After a considerable battle to get through to the finish, the Italians were awarded the top honours for a second time.

Eight countries sent two teams each to take part in the 1985 event, which took the vehicles across the jungle-covered mountains of Borneo. For the second year running equatorial rainstorms were the major enemy, and at one stage a helicopter airlift had to be arranged for all the vehicles, or the competition would have come to a premature halt. The overall expedition trophy was won by the originators of the event, West Germany, but a new Team Spirit Award was introduced for the first time, and this went to the Brazilian team of Rosenberg and Probst. the new award replaced the recognition of overall teamwork that was lost when the major trophy went to high achievers in the Special Tasks section.

Further and faster

By contrast to the nightmarish conditions that delayed and nearly stopped the Borneo expedition, the 1986 Camel Trophy was the longest and fastest in the event's history. Fourteen nations each entered a two-man team, and the vehicles had to negotiate a 2000-mile trail through Australia's Northern Territories. The whole thing was completed in just 13 days, despite a delay of 24 hours while the crews built rafts to get the convoy across a swollen river. The French had entered a team for the first time, and they were declared the overall winners when the expedition reached Darwin. The Team Spirit Award was handed to the home-based Australian crew.

For 1987 the event moved due west across the Indian Ocean to Madagascar – a country with such difficult terrain that few roads or railways exist outside the major centres of population. Again 14 teams contested the trophy, this time in Range Rover turbocharged diesels. The expedition completed the first ever north to south traverse of the island, covering over 1400 miles in the process. Italy took the major trophy for the third time in six years, while Spain collected the Team Spirit Award.

The overall format of the competition was slightly changed in 1988, with two distinct Special Task stages being put in at the beginning and end of the actual expedition. In some ways this was a reflection of the event's enormous publicity appeal, because it gave the ever-growing press corps something to look at and photograph, without them having to suffer the privations of actually joining the expedition in the mud. This is a difficult situation to resolve. Undoubtedly a big press attendance will change the character of an event like the Camel Trophy, because photo-opportunities and the like must be provided for, both in the event budget and in its timetable. This is probably unpopular with the teams and support personnel – especially at the end of the expedition when they are physically exhausted anyway – but they have to recognize that without publicity there would be no funds for the competition in the first place. The new format did at least mean that the 12 teams were able to profit more fully from the 1300 mile uninterrupted adventure drive across the formidable mountain and jungle regions of Sulawesi – perhaps the least well known of the Indonesian islands. The overall event was won by Turkey, but the UK team of Marc Day and Jim Benson received the Team Spirit Award.

Ten Years on

The organizers of the Camel Trophy decided to celebrate its tenth anniversary by returning to Brazil for the 1989 competition, and the steamy Amazon Jungle provided the main expedition route for perhaps the toughest event yet. Fourteen different national crews toiled day and night to pull the convoy through seemingly endless mud, and at times their rate of progress barely exceeded two or three kilometres a day. None of the competitors are likely to forget the event, particularly the moment that they broke free of almost impenetrable undergrowth to get their first sight of the mighty Amazon river. It was certainly a rare moment of pleasure for brothers Joe and Bob Ives, who managed to haul their Land Rover through to become the first British winners of the big trophy.

As the competition moved towards its second decade, political walls were beginning to crumble all over Europe – and this opened up new opportunities to site the event away from equatorial regions for the first time. After a considerable period of research and negotiation, it was announced that the 1990 Camel Trophy would become the first major international motoring event to be held in the Soviet Union – a considerable coup for the organizing team. The Land Rover Discovery vehicle was used in competition for the first time, and 16 national teams – the biggest field ever – took part in the event.

The course took them from the formal starting ceremony in Bratsk, south-east through the infamous Taiga Forest to Lake Baikal, and then south-west to the regional capital of Irkutsk: over 1000 miles through some of the most spectacular and varied terrain ever encountered during the expedition phase of the event. There were 14 Special Tasks to be completed on the way, with a maximum available score of 336 points for each competing team (24 points for each Task win). The Dutch pair of Stijn Luykx and Rob Kamps achieved a magnificent total of 249 points to win the event, with Germany second and the United Kingdom team of Andrew Dacey and Richard Tomlinson, third. The Team Spirit Award was presented to the ever-helpful pair from the Canary Islands.

How it all comes together

The Camel Trophy is an annual event, organized and funded by the marketing division of R. J. Reynolds International. A full-time staff of about 20 is responsible for arranging and managing the expedition, but many others – from both inside and outside the company – devote a substantial amount of their time to the big event. The overall planning team is permanently based in the United Kingdom, at the Reynolds' offices in Woking, Surrey.

Decisions about the location of each event have to be taken at least a year in advance. Official Camel Trophy scout teams visit the selected areas to obtain all the necessary diplomatic clearances, survey the route alternatives and confirm the shipping and logistical requirements. This is no easy task for a convoy of about 30 vehicles, carrying competitors and support personnel from many different nations. As soon as the fine details are broadly fixed, the location can be formally announced and applications for team places invited.

The vehicles involved are chosen by the Trophy management organization, and then purchased by Reynolds in the normal way: this allows a degree of independence of choice that would not be available if the event entered into a long-term contract with any one vehicle manufacturer. Apart from the first expedition (which used AMC Jeeps), Land Rover and Range Rover vehicles have been used in various combinations every year. The competitors are provided wth identical vehicles, equipped to the same standards for every team. The mix of support vehicles can vary depending on their basic task during the event.

All the competition vehicles are normal production models, built to the same standards as those in any high-street showroom. They are, however, modified to incorporate specific expedition-related equipment. The 1990 Discovery TDis were fitted with a full roll-cage that actually incorporated the roof-rack, which gave the vehicle strength enough to resist the possible crushing forces of a multiple roll-over (down a steep slope for instance). Safety planning on this scale is essential for such difficult and unknown terrain. The sump guard was slightly extended to protect the steering linkages, and the fuel tank was also protected by a stiff undertray. Nudge bars were fitted, and each vehicle was equipped with four roof-mounted spotlamps and a high-intensity 'reversing' lamp. The engine air inlet was raised to roof level to keep it well clear of any water, and an exhaust-powered Air-Lift jacking system was provided this year instead of the 'traditional' Hi-Lift. All the vehicles were fitted with Husky electric winches, and each carried a supply of ropes, snatch-blocks, pulleys, tree-strops and shackles. Ground anchors, an axe and a pick and shovel were also included as standard equipment. The tyres on the competition vehicles were all 700x16 Michelin XCLs.

Each member of the crew was allowed to take only 25 kilos (55 lb) of 'personal' baggage, which

FOUR WHEEL DRIVING

included all food and clothing! Positively sealed plastic boxes were provided to keep these things dry, but everything else had to take its chances behind the rear compartment grille. The vehicles were all equipped with two tents and four sleeping bags, which would provide accommodation for the crew, and for the nationally-sponsored journalists that often accompany the competing teams throughout the event.

Nearly two million people appplied to join the 1990 event, most of them through their own national organizers, but some direct to the Surrey headquarters. From this massive quantity of application forms (every one is looked at closely), about 30 from each country are chosen to go forward into the selection trials. Each country normally runs its own selection process, but two or three national teams can join forces to make better use of the available facilities. The British trials for the 1990 event, which were held at an Army training ground near Camberley, were also joined by the Swiss and Austrian candidates.

The selection trials are extremely demanding events in their own right. The candidates are expected to live under canvas no matter what the weather, and complete exhausting tasks at any time of the day or night, often in the pouring rain and at a moment's notice. The organizers are looking for the sort of personal endurance that can help to pull a Land Rover 127 support vehicle (weighing about four tons) out of a bottomless bog; or put an overturned One-Ten ambulance back on its wheels, only to spend the next two hours up to one's knees in a fast-flowing Arctic river trying to get the engine going again! Both of these little adventures happened on the 1990 event in Siberia.

Of the 30 UK hopefuls that attended the Camberley weekend, only 12 were selected to go on to the

CAMEL TROPHY

ABOVE AND LEFT
How not to drive through water, 'assist' the diff lock or stow your winch wire! Then again, you're not competing in the Camel Trophy – yet.

ABOVE
Previous experiences of collapsing roof racks during the Madagascar event led to their incorporation into the roll-cage for 1990.

next stage – a three-day mini safari at the Duke of Somerset's Maiden Bradley estate in Wiltshire. This stage of the competition whittled the numbers down to just four people, who went on to the full international trials weekend just outside Paris.

The competition for the two national places is obviously intense. The event is open to men and women over the age of 21, but you must have a valid driving licence and be fairly fit. The selection is aimed solely at amateurs, so if you have ever held an RAC competitions licence you cannot qualify for Camel Trophy.

The 1991 event is hosted by the two East African states of Tanzania and Burundi. At the time of writing, entries were recorded from 17 nations. The 18-day expedition is to follow the explorer David Livingstone's route to the source of the Nile. 23 Discoverys and 13 Defender 110s were shipped out for the expedition from Dar es Salaam to Bujumbura on the shores of Lake Tanganyika.

13
The Ultimate Dirty Weekend?

'You'll have to stop at the bottom so I can open the gate' said Ronnie Dale in his soft, matter of fact, Scottish burr from the other side of the Range Rover cab.

'Oh yeah?' I thought, 'how the hell are we going to do that?'

The gate in question was directly in front of me, at the bottom of a steep, slippery grass slope that we were slowly descending in low range first gear. Simply maintaining control under those conditions was a chancy business, but the thought of actually stopping put my brain into overdrive. There was nowhere to stop safely, and no run-off area that would enable us to alter course before nearly two tons of Range Rover Vogue inflicted grievous bodily harm on itself, and on a perfectly innocent five-bar gate.

Ronnie grinned knowingly, and my companion Fiona giggled from the back seat, thoroughly amused by my predicament. If I used the footbrake we would quickly lose grip and toboggan right through the gate (accompanied by some awful crunching noises), and the handbrake was out of bounds because it would damage the transmission system. In sheer desperation I reached for the key and turned the ignition off, uttering a silent prayer as I did so. Everything went beautifully quiet as the big 2.4 litre diesel engine died, and we rolled to a halt only inches short of the very solid-looking gate. I allowed myself a moment or two of smug self-congratulation, but inside I felt like a little boy who'd stopped a runaway train just seconds from disaster.

Ronnie and Trish Dale are particularly proud of their Off-Road Adventure Driving School – and with considerable justification. Nestling in the softly rolling Lammermuir Hills, just south of Edinburgh, the school provides an ideal environment for beginners who want to get a feel for off-road driving, or for experienced drivers who just want to play, or brush-up particular skills under the watchful eye and quiet patience of one of Britain's leading off-road drivers.

Ronnie had had two years of off-road driver training with the highly regarded Land Rover Demonstration Team, and had been chosen as a UK finalist in the selection trials for the arduous Camel Trophy event. Throughout the period of rapid growth in the popularity of 4WD vehicles, he recognized that there was a place in the market for a centre offering not only skilled tuition for beginners, but also a purpose-built course that would enable even professional drivers to sharpen up their skills without inflicting further damage on an already overstretched landscape.

The school was launched at the 'Off-Road Scotland' show in 1987, and is now firmly established as one of the best in the business. Land was not a particular problem for Ronnie because he already ran a successful dairy farm. He set aside a few acres of unproductive pasture to build a course that would be taxing, but safe for every level of experience. Some of the obstacles he has created are daunting even to the most skilful of drivers, but the whole emphasis of the place has been on safety right from the start, and no one is pushed into taking any unnecessary risks.

New members welcome

Off-road driving schools are a relatively recent phenomenon in Great Britain, and I had been interested in attending one ever since I first heard about them. The preparation of this book gave me an ideal opportunity to discover something about the philosophy behind these schools, and to watch one in action. I particularly wanted to see how a novice driver would fare after some expert tuition,

THE ULTIMATE DIRTY WEEKEND?

ABOVE
Fizz indulges in some mud slinging as she blasts her way into the purpose-built trough. Not the correct way to enter water! (P.T.O)

LEFT
Always prepare your approach angles properly before you go out to play – especially when you're in someone else's vehicle – or you too will have a bent number plate.

113

FOUR WHEEL DRIVING

ABOVE
Now that's better!
Drive in slowly, and
gently push the water
into a nice bow-wave.

RIGHT
Having demolished
one bollard already,
a novice descends a very
slippery slope with the
back end beginning to
break away again. Time
to accelerate slightly
to bring it back into line.

THE ULTIMATE DIRTY WEEKEND?

ABOVE
The 'see-saw' was designed to simulate a camel-hump ridge.

LEFT
Driving with only one set of wheels on the see-saw allows you to explore some interesting roll angles.

115

FOUR WHEEL DRIVING

but I also wanted to find out how much I *really* knew about off-road driving, and whether a reasonably experienced driver could benefit from a period of concentrated training.

Transport for the occasion was gallantly provided by Land Rover Ltd, who kindly loaned me a Range Rover Vogue Turbo diesel for two weeks. As an expatriate Scotsman, the opportunity to spend Hogmanay in a part of Britain that I love, with plenty of off-roading, a Range Rover Vogue and a blonde, female companion (probably in that order!), was simply irresistible – perhaps the ultimate dirty weekend!

My blonde companion and novice driver was a long-suffering friend called Fiona – known as Fizz to all her friends. Apart from sharing my love for off-road driving, Fizz is also a keen photographer and was foolhardy enough to volunteer for a cold, wet weekend in Scotland, where she would probably spend most of her time ankle-deep in mud.

Sure enough, the Saturday of our visit dawned cold and overcast, with a definite threat of rain later – perfect off-roading conditions. Fizz had been detailed to spend the morning riding in Ronnie's Land Rover 90 with another pupil called Harry. This would give her an opportunity to see at first hand how the tuition worked, before she was let loose in the Range Rover. Being unfamiliar with the course, I decided to follow them around the 'nursery-slopes' section. This consisted of a number of steep ascents and descents, sideslopes and water splashes, all designed to help the novice drive with increasing confidence, using the gearbox to its maximum effect. Particular care was taken over the handling of aborted ascents, and a substantial amount of time was devoted to the correct use of clutch and brake pedals during these potentially hazardous manoeuvres. This was just one illustration of the priority given to safety during every period of tuition.

The *pièce de résistance* in the nursery-slopes area was a specially constructed 'see-saw'. Designed to test a driver's reflexes and sense of balance, this fiendish device proved remarkably difficult to master. Basically it simulates a camel-hump, and a very fast change-down into low-range first is needed just as the platform pivots over with the advancing weight of the vehicle. On more than one occasion I skated down the other side completely out of control – either stuck hopelessly in neutral or frantically trying to find first! I put all this down to an unreasonably stiff gearbox – but the others chuckled and were a good deal less generous.

The remarkable see-saw was also used to familiarize a driver with the increasing roll-angle on a difficult sideslope. The trick here was to drive with one set of fore-and-aft wheels on the ramp, and the other set running alongside on the ground. The net effect is to gradually tilt the vehicle to about 35 degrees. This was great fun, but the pivoting action of the platform, combined with the rapidly changing tilt angle, produced some entertaining feedback from the suspension units. Not to be recommended if you suffer from seasickness.

Our new friend Harry, who normally drives a Volkswagen Golf GTi, proved a very able pupil and we soon moved across into the boggy stuff. This was where the fun really started. The area contained many short and steep ascents and descents into and out of flowing watercourses, and everything was very slippery. I was soon having a thoroughly enjoyable time playing in the mud, only coming to grief once when I grounded the Range Rover cresting the top of a hill. Harry kindly came to the rescue and pulled me free with the Land Rover.

After an excellent lunch in the farmhouse (with lots of off-road talk) we swapped places and Ronnie took Fizz off in the Range Rover for her lesson. I spent the afternoon driving a new prototype 4 × 4, and chasing Fizz around the course trying to get some pictures. Under Ronnie's watchful eye she was soon driving like an expert, and enjoying herself so much that I spent the rest of the weekend trying to prise the Rover's keys out of her sticky little paws!

Sunday morning saw Fizz being ejected from the nice warm cab and told to do her bit with the cameras, while I got down to some serious playing in a 2000-acre forest that the school has access to. This was the highlight of the whole weekend for me. The forest had some 40 miles of rough track, most of it on steep slopes that must have been close to 45 degrees at times. There were plenty of camel-humps, obstacles and river crossings to test both the vehicle and the driver, and it proved to be an absolute paradise for a keen off-roader. The whole area offered some of the toughest terrain I had ever driven across.

During this section a punctured nearside front tyre caused a bit of excitement. Having chocked the vehicle, extracted the spare wheel and jacked up

THE ULTIMATE DIRTY WEEKEND?

nearly two tons of Range Rover, we realized that we had no wheel-brace to undo the nuts! What a masterpiece of preparation that was. After exchanging some quite unprintable language, we were forced to re-pack everything and drive 400 ft back down through the forest, before hi-jacking a passing farmer. Luckily he was able to help, so we did manage to complete our excursion, but I shall check my took kit much more carefully in future.

A good shortcut

On Sunday afternoon, with the New Year celebrations only a few hours away, we took the final photographs and had a last play in the bog before cleaning the Range Rover in readiness for our long journey back to the South of England. It was with great sadness that we headed home after a really memorable weekend.

I came away convinced that these specialist schools have a very important role to play in the expanding world of off-road driving. Under the patient and kindly tuition of Ronnie Dale, my novice had become a fully-fledged off-road driver, with the skills and anticipation to master almost any situation that might be thrown at her in the future. I was personally surprised by how much I had learned, and how much further I had pushed my own limits – although driving along a narrow track 200 ft above a raging river did little to cure my vertigo!

For those of you with your own 4WD vehicle the centre offers a marvellous opportunity to have considerable fun in complete safety. If you don't currently own a suitable vehicle, Ronnie can offer a Mercedes G-Wagen as well as the Land Rover 90 turbocharged diesel. If you feel really adventurous, he also has Quad-Bikes that you can ride around on, or even a single-seat hovercraft. Now that does sound like fun!

The school's flowing water courses provide an interesting challenge for any pupil.

The Off-Roader's Directory

Off-Road Clubs

Compiled with the assistance of *Off Road and 4 Wheel Drive* magazine.

Rover Clubs

Association of Rover Clubs Ltd.
Hon Sec: Andrew Stavordale, 65 Longmead Avenue, Hazel Grove, Stockport, Cheshire SK7 5PJ

Breckland Land Rover Club Ltd.
Mrs Carol Roberts, Beck Cottage, Swafield, North Walsham, Norfolk NR28 0QX

Cornwall & Devon Land Rover Club.
Mrs Marion Rolstone, 64 Sunnybanks, Saltash, Cornwall PL12 6SA

Cumbrian Land Rover Club
Peter Anstiss, 4 Blucoat Crescent, Newton-with-Scales, Preston, Lancs PR4 3TJ

Dorset LR & RR Owners' Club
Pam Wells, The Cross, Belschawell, Blandford Forum, Dorset DT11 0EG

Essex Land Rover Club
Dave Bygrave, The Knoll, Bygrave Road, Ashwell, Nr Baldock, Herts SG7 5RH

101 FC Club
Peter Wardley, Suite 2, Perton Centre, Perton, Wolverhampton WV6 7QH

Hants & Berks Rover Owners' Club
Gary Hodgson, 5 Beckham Lane, Petersfield, Hants GU32 3BU

Lancashire & Cheshire Rover Owners' Club
Ian Foster, 31 Slimbridge Close, Breightmet, Bolton BL2 5NT

Land Rover Register (1947–1951)
Mrs Sally Cooknell, Langford Cottage, School Lane, Ladbroke, Leamington Spa, Warks CV33 0BX

Land Rover Series One Club
David Bowyer, East Foldhay, Zeal Monachorum, Crediton, Devon EX17 6DH

Land Rover Series Two Club
Ross Floyd, PO Box 1609, Yatton, Bristol BS19 4QP

Lincolnshire Land Rover Club
Steve Wells, 6 Hall Farm Cottage, Binbrook, Lincolnshire LN3 6BW

Midland Rover Owners' Club
Derek Spooner, Bank Cottage, Abbots Morton, Worcestershire WR7 4NA

Newcastle and Nantwich Rover Owners' Club
M. R. Griffiths, 39 New Road, Madeley, Nr Crewe, Cheshire CW3 9HD

North Eastern Rover Owners' Club
Mrs June Green, 248 Horsely Road, Barmiston, Washington, Tyne & Wear NE38 8HP

North Wales Land Rover Club
Mrs Pauline Morris, The Filling Station, Pentrefoelas Rd, Bylchau, Denbigh, Clwyd LL16 5LS

Peak & Dukeries Land Rover Club
Mrs P. Beecham, 8 Bridge End Avenue, Selston, Notts NG16 6BE

Pennine Land Rover Club
Mrs Ann Whittaker, 121 Brown Lodge Drive, Smithy Bridge, Littleborough, Lancs OL15 0ET

Range Rover Register Ltd.
Chris Tomley, Cwm Cochen, Bettws, Newtown, Powys SY16 3LQ

THE OFF-ROADER'S DIRECTORY

Red Rose Land Rover Club
W. E. D. Ryan, 148 Higher Walton Road, Walton le Dale, Preston PR5 4HR

Scottish Land Rover Owners' Club
Bob Webster, 1 Hallyards Farm Cottages, Kirkliston, EH29 9DZ

Somerset & Wiltshire Rover Owners' Club
Peter Usher, The New Garage, Dursley Road, Trowbridge, Wiltshire BA14 0NW

Southern Rover Owners' Club
Tracey McCartney, 314 Broadwalk, Blackheath, London SE3 8NH

Staffordshire & Shropshire LR Club
Mrs V. S. Johnson, 4 Waltham House, Overend Street, West Bromwich, West Midlands B70 6ER

Wye & Welsh Rover Owners' Club
Peter Thomas, 1 Bracelands Drive, Christchurch, Colford, Gloucestershire GL16 7NN

Yorkshire Rover Owners' Club
Mrs Sue Whiteley, 10 Thorncliffe, Kirburton, Huddersfield HD8 0UG

For the ultimate in road-legal off-road machinery, discard the body of your old Range Rover and bolt-on the Rage Rover buggy kit.

Other Clubs

All Wheel Drive Club
David Sarsfield-Hall, Flat 6, 85 Henley Road, Caversham, Reading, Berks RG4 0DS

Anglian Rover Owners' Club Ltd.
Tim Northend, 219 Whaddon Way, Bletchley, Milton Keynes MK3 7oZ

The Austin Gipsy Register
Mike Gilbert, 24 Green Close, Sturminster Newton, Dorset DT10 1BJ

Buchan Off-Road Drivers' Club
Eddie McConochie, 15 Slains Crescent, Cruden Bay, Peterhead, Aberdeenshire

FOUR WHEEL DRIVING

The remarkable full-time 4WD RTV has a lockable swivel between the forward-control cab and the load space, which allows it to clamber into the most awkward places. The vehicle is powered by a Ford diesel engine, coupled to an automatic transmission system.

Cleveland 4WD Club
Ernie Graves, 71 Barrington Crescent, Thorntree Est, Middlesborough, Cleveland.

The Deeside Four Wheel Drive Club
Lorraine Allen, c/o Banchory Lodge Hotel, Banchory, Kincardineshire AB3 3HS

East Devon Off-Road Club
Mrs Wendy Arnold, Birch House, Clayhidon, Cullompton, Devon

East Midlands Off-Road Club
M. Jacques, Woodstock, Gainsborough Road, Winthorpe, Newark, Notts NG24 2NN

Forward Control Register 11A & 11B
CB Heron, 28 Front Street, Daisy Hill, Sacriston, Co Durham, DH7 6BL

Haflinger Owners' Club
Ashley Simpkins, 50 The Saintfield, Tewkesbury, Gloucestershire GL20 8RU

Highland 4WD Club
DG Meiklejohn, Gask Farmhouse, Farr, Inverness IV1 2XD

Isle of Wight 4 × 4 Club
M. J. Penketh, 75 Church Road, Wootton, Isle of Wight PO33 4PZ

Jeep Owners' Association
Ron Bean, 1 Chiltern Road, Dunstable, Bedfordshire LU6 1EP

Jeep Owners' Register
Chris & Val Bailey, 252 Lon Pinwydd, Trehafren, Newtown, Powys SY16 1QF

Midland Offroad Club
Charles Deverill, 26 The Cotswolds, Alvechurch Highway, Lydiate Ash, Bromsgrove, Worcs

Mid Wales Four-Wheel Drive Club
Jenny Dee, Erwyd Garage, Ponterwyd, Aberystwyth

Military Vehicle Trust
Nigel Godfrey, 6 Brackenbury, The Drove, Andover, Hants SP10 3PU

National 39/45 Military Vehicle Group
Nick Peters, 18 Preston Close, Stanton-u-Bardon, Leicestershire

National Niva Owners' Club
Shirley Sharman, 12 Paddock Close, Clapham, Bedford.

National Off Road Association
Kevin Moody, 7 Church Lane, Castle Donington, Derbyshire DE7 2LG

Northern Ireland Four Wheel Drive Club
Ian Henderson, 12 Abbot View, Bowtown Est, Newtownards, Co Down, Northern Ireland BT23 3XT

Northern Off-Road Club
Margaret Marlow, 2 Moor View, Bingley Road, Menston, Nr Ilkley, West Yorkshire LS29 6BD

Southern Counties Off-Roaders
Jane Dooley, 149 Slepe Crescent, Parkstone, Poole, Dorset BH12 4DL

Subaru Owners Club
Ralph Sillett, Subaru (UK) Ltd, Ryder Street, West Bromwich, W Midlands B70 0EJ

Suffolk 4-Wheel Drive Club
Maureen Lyes, 2 Thelnetham Road, Blo Norton, Diss, Norfolk IP22 2JQ

Suzuki Rhino Club
Ian Catford, Suzuki GB (Cars) Ltd, 46 Gatwick Road, Crawley, West Sussex RH10 2XF

Viking Off-Road Club
John Taylor, Fearn House, 1 Guilford Drive, Wigston Fields, Leicestershire LE8 1HG

West Wales 4 × 4 Group
D Iwan Jenkins, Rofft, Aberporth, Cardigan, Dyfed SA4 3DF

Expedition Preparation and Planning

Overlanders Club
Impala House, 34–38 Victoria Road, Horley, Surrey RH6 7PZ

Overland Ltd.
Link Road, West Wilts Trading Estate, Westbury, Wiltshire BA13 4JB

K & J Slavin (Quest) Ltd.
Cow Pasture Farm, Louth Road, Hainton, Lincolnshire LN3 6LX

Guided Expeditions and Off-road Adventure Holidays

Eagle Land Rover Expeditions
55 Glen Nevis, East Kilbride, Scotland

Neil Hopkinson African Off-road Safaris
Dairy Cottage, Knightcote, Warwickshire CV33 0SE

Northern Safaris
121 Goodshaw Lane, Goodshaw, Rossendale, Lancashire BB4 8DJ

Off-road Driver Training Schools

Colzie Hill Recreation
Easter Colzie, Auchtermuchty, Fife, Scotland

Mr K. Conway
57 Easterly Close, Brackla, Bridgend, Mid-Glamorgan, South Wales

The Ronnie Dale Off-Road Adventure Driving School
Whiteburn, Abbey St Bathans, Duns, Berwickshire TD11 3RU, Scotland

FOUR WHEEL DRIVING

The Great Challenge Company
Old Crossford, Moniaive by Thornhill, Dumfries & Galloway DG– 4DZ

Highland Drovers
Croft of Kincardine, Boat of Garten, Invernesshire PH24 3BY, Scotland

Mr S. Johnson
Speel Bank Farm, Cartmel, Grange-over-Sands, Cumbria LA11 7Sp

Steve Jolly Autos
High Street, Leek, Staffordshire

The Overlander Off-Road School
East Foldhay, Zeal Monachorum, Nr Crediton, Devon EX17 6DH

Rough Terrain Training Centre
36 Hinton Road, Woodford Halse, Daventry, Northants

Thumbs Up Off Roading
Tredington Cross Roads, Shipston-on-Stour, Warwickshire CV36 4NN

Warwickshire College of Agriculture
Off-road Driving School, Moreton Morrell, Warwickshire CV35 9BL

Accessory Suppliers

Land Rover/Range Rover/Discovery Vehicles

ASG (Accessories) Ltd.
Sandown Road, Derby DE2 8SR

Aylmer Motor Works Ltd.
Unit 2, St George's Industrial Estate, White Hart Lane, London N22 5QL

Roger M. Bass
Curtiss Mill Green, Stapleford Tawney, Romford, Essex RM4 1RT

Bearmach (London) Ltd.
Maindy Road, Cardiff, South Wales CF2 4XN

Central Garage
Middleton-on-the-Wolds, Driffield, North Humberside YO25 9UA

4 Wheel Drive Truck Centre
Haresigns Garage, Gosberton Risegate, Nr Spalding, Lincs PE11 4EZ

Land Ranger Services Ltd.
Unit 1c, Brooks Lane Industrial Estate, Middlewich, Cheshire CW10 0JG

RW Leng Land Rovers
Juniperbank, Walkerbank, Peebleshire EH43 6DE, Scotland

Lovell Land Rovers
Westminster Industrial Estate, Station Road, North Hykeham, Lincs LN6 3QY

Nicholas Paxton
The Workshop, Cloford, Nr Frome, Somerset BA11 4PM

Rimmer Bros Ltd.
Triumph House, 115 Lincoln Road, Branston, Lincs LN4 1PX

RJ Land Rovers
179 Hophouse Cottages, Duddlestone, Tauton, Somerset TA3 7BW

Shaw Contract Services Ltd.
Old Road, Alderbury, Salisbury, Wiltshire SP5 3AR

Southern Counties Garages
Discovery House, 13–15 London Road, Crawley, West Sussex RH10 2JG

Stafford Land Rover Centre
Island Garage, Lichfield, Stafforshire ST17 4JU

Three Counties Land Rovers
Boddington Road, Byfield, Nr Daventry, Northamptonshire NN11 6XU

Windmill Service Station
Preston New Road, Mellor, Nr Blackburn, Lancashire BB2 7PU

Other makes of vehicle

Colin Appleyard Cars (*Suzuki*)
Cornmill Garage, Hilifax Road, Keighley, West Yorkshire BD21 1AH

Belgravia Garage (*Toyota*)
126–132 High Street, Tooting, London SW17 0RR

THE OFF-ROADER'S DIRECTORY

Cheam Motors (Ewell) Ltd. (*Subaru, Isuzu*)
4–8 Cheam Road, Ewell, Surrey KT17 1SN

Colmar Motor Engineers Ltd. (*Portaro Pampas*)
8 Vanguard Trading Estate, Seaforth Lane, Chesterfield, Derbyshire S40 2TZ

Cross Roads Garage (*Subaru, Isuzu, Toyota, Mitsubishi, Suzuki*)
Tredington, Shipston-on-Stour, Warwickshire CV36 4NN

EARS 4 × 4 Centre (*All makes*)
9 Lord Street, Macclesfield, Cheshire SK11 6SY

Gordon Motors (*Suzuki*)
Comrie Road, Crieff, Perthshire PH7 4BQ

Highfield Garage (Winchmore Hill) Ltd. (*Suzuki*)
Westpole Avenue, Cockfosters, Barnet, Hertfordshie EN4 OBN

Kamshaft Durham (*Suzuki*)
Abbey Road Industrial Estate, Pity Me, County Durham DH1 5HA

The Supacat is a Volkswagen diesel-powered 6WD amphibious vehicle with automatic transmission. One of the most agile machines in its class, the handlebar-controlled skid steering operates on all six wheels, while the front four only have an additional ackerman system.

Kamshaft Sunderland (*Suzuki*)
Wessington Way, Castleton, Sunderland SR5 3NS

Lada Cars (*Lada Niva*)
Western House, Middle Lane, Wythall, Birmingham B47 6LA

Leisure Accessories Ltd. (*Alloy Wheels*)
Britannia Works, Hurricane Way, Airport Ind Est, Norwich, Norfolk NR6 6EY

Pro-Speed Off-Road & Race Equipment (*All makes*)
14 Woodside Road, Lenton Abbey, Nottingham NG9 2TL

Quicksilver Automotive
11–15 Stoney Lake, Sparkbrook, Birmingham B12 8DL

Tungston Ltd. (*Isuzu*)
Finchley Central, London N3 1RJ

Up-Country Autoproducts UK Ltd. (*All makes*)
Howard Works, Norwich Road, Halesworth, Suffolk IP19 8QH

White Horse Motors (*Toyota, Daihatsu, Nissan, Suzuki*)
Whitestone, Nr Exeter, Devon EX6 6EH

PE Wilson (Autos Ltd. (*Toyota*)
1171 High Road, Chadwell Heath, Romford, Essex RM6 4AL

Parts and Spares Suppliers

Land Rover/Range Rover/Discovery Vehicles

Autosport Ltd.
Unit 20, Zennor Road Trading Estate, Off Weir Road, London SW12 0RS

Candol
Bansons Yard, High Street, Ongar, Essex CM5 9AA

CLASP (Scunthorpe) Ltd.
163 Moorwell Road Industrial Estate, Scunthorpe, Sth Humberside DN17 2SX

John Craddock Ltd.
70–76 North Street, Bridgetown, Cannock, Staffordshire

Droitwich Garage Ltd.
St Georges Square, Droitwich, Worcestershire WR9 8LD

Keith Gott Land Rovers
Tailgates, Hogmoor Road, Bordon, Hants GU35 9HL

Kenning Derby
Derwent Street, Derby DE1 2EF

Land Rover Centre
Bridge Street, Lockwood, Huddersfield, Yorkshire HD4 6EL

Land Rover Replacements
Clarks Hill, Storrs Hill Road, Ossett, Yorkshire

Lex
Bell Lane, Bury, Manchester BL9 6DJ

Lex
Princess Way, Cheltenham, Gloucestershire GL51 7RB

Lex
128 Bridge Road, Maidenhead, Berkshire SL6 8DD

Lex
Morris House, Shaftesbury Street, Newport, Gwent NP9 5XS, South Wales

Lex
150 Stourbridge Road, Lye, Stourbridge, West Midlands DY9 7BU

Mayborn Engineering Services
Ironmould Lane, Brislington, Bristol BS4 4TZ

Peterborough Four Wheel Drive
Point Two Four, Newark Road, Peterborough PE1 5UA

Rovercare
37 Aylmer Parade, Aylmer Road, London N20 0PE

Shukers Ltd.
New Road, Ludlow, Shropshire SY8 2LS

David Simmonite
755 Thornton Road, Thornton, Bradford, Yorkshire BD1 3NW

SMT.
1 Kerr Street, Greenock, Inverclyde, Scotland

Tannery Farm Garage
Elephant Lane, St Helens, Merseyside WA9 5EP

Wadham Kenning Motor Group Ltd.
Callywhite Lane, Dronfield, Yorkshire S18 6XP

Woburn Abbey Garage
London Road, Woburn, Milton Keynes MK17 9PY

Roger Young Land Rover Centre
Ninestones, Nr Bolventor, Liskeard, Cornwall PL14 6SD

Roger Young Land Rover Service Centre
Rosevear Road Ind Est, St Austell Road, Bugle, St Austell, Cornwall

THE OFF-ROADER'S DIRECTORY

Other Vehicles

CARS Sales & Hire Ltd. (*Isuzu, Subaru, Land Rover, Range Rover*)
The Garage, Aldeburgh, Friston, Suffolk IP17 1NP

Country Vehicle Services (*UMM Transcat, ARO, Dacia, Nissan conversions*)
Livingshayes, Silverton, Exeter, Devon

Reg Hill Ltd. (*Suzuki*)
Branch End Garage, Gildersome, Morely, Nr Leeds, Yorkshire LS27 7LL

Specialist Suppliers

Andover Vehicle Services (*BMW Diesel conversions for Range Rover*)
114 Commercial Centre, Picket Piece, Andover, Hampshire SP11 6LU

Chatsworth Motor Spares Ltd. (*Carburettor and performance conversions for Range Rover*)
362 Chatsworth Road, Chesterfield, Derbyshire

The MWG 8WD all-terrain vehicle is based on Land Rover 110 parts. It can carry a crew of 4-5 people plus a good-sized load, and can go almost anywhere a tank can go.

DPR Ltd (*Performance conversions for Range Rover*)
Watercombe Lane, Lynx Trading Estate, Yeovill, Somerset

DVS Land Rovers (*Land Rover restoration and transmission specialists*)
84 Oakdene Road, Brockham, Betchworth, Surrey RH3 7JX

Essex Turbocharging (*Suppliers and servicing of all makes of turbocharger*)
Causeway Industrial Estate, Galliford Road, Maldon, Essex CM9 7XD

JE Motors Ltd. (*Performance conversions for Range Rover/Discovery*)
Unit 4, New Era Ind Est, Siskin Drive, Coventry, West Midlands CV3 4FJ

Mercia 4 × 4 Engineering (*Isuzu turbo Diesel conversions for Land Rover/Range Rover*)
Unit 4, Cannock Ind Centre, Walkmill Lane, Bridgetown, Cannock WS11 3LN

Merlin Automotive Developments (*Cabriolet conversions for Range Rovers*)
Hendall Gate Farm, Herons Ghyll, East Sussex TN22 4BU

Motor & Diesel Engineering (*Mazda Diesel conversions for Land Rover/Range Rover*)
Station Works, Old North Road, Bourn, Cambridge CB3 7TZ

Norfolk Land Rover Centre (*Nissan Diesel conversions for Land Rover/Range Rover*)
Rushall, Diss, Nofolk.

Steve Parker Land Rovers (*Ford V6 conversion kits for Land Rovers*)
Unit 72, Healey Halls Mils, Healey Dell, Rochdale, Lancs OL12 6BG

Pontuir Tyre Services (*Specialist off-road tyre retailer*)
Unit 3, Boxer Trading Estate, Pontuir Road, Caerleon, Gwent NP6 1NY

RT Quaife Engineering Ltd. (*Self-locking differentials for 4 × 4 and light commercial vehicles*)
Botany Industrial Estate, Sovereign Way, Tonbridge, Kent TN9 1RS

Rapid Rovers (*Specialist conversions to owners' requirements. Builders of racing and trials vehicles*)
Dean Farm, Kingsley, Bordon, Hants GU35 9NG

Alvin Smith Range Rovers (*Performance conversions for Land Rover/Range Rover/Discovery vehicles. Builders of specialist off-road racing vehicles*)
Smiths Garage, Wallis Wood, Dorking, Surrey RH5 5RD

Surrey Off-Road Specialists Ltd.
(*Dick Cepek Tyres, ARB Air Locker differentials. Specialist vehicle conversions to owners' requirements*)
25A Hewitts Industrial Estate, Cranleigh, Surrey GU6 8LW

TB Turbo (*Turbo conversions for most 4WD vehicles*)
Port Royal Avenue, Off Willow Lane, Lune Ind Est, Lancaster LA1 5QP

Turner Engineering (*Complete range of re-manufactured Land Rover/Range Rover engines*)
Churchill House, West Park Road, Newchapel, Nr Lingfield, Surrey RH7 6HT

Warwick Banks Handling (*Performance and handling kits for Range Rover*)
West Farm, Witham-on-the-Hill, Bourne, Lincolnshire PE10 0JN

Watson & Turner (*Diesel conversions for Land Rover/Range Rover*)
18 Diamond Street, Heaviley, Stockport, Manchester SK2 6PQ

Specialist off-road Vehicle Manufactures

Foers Engineering (*IBEX – Land Rover/Range Rover based 4WD*)
Gateway Industrial Estate, The Gateway, Rotherham, Sth Yorkshire S62 6JL

MWG All Terrain Vehicles (*MWG 8 × 8 – Land Rover 110 based vehicle*)
MWG House, Hanworth Lane, Chertsey, Surrey KT16 9LA

Overland Ltd (*Pinzgauer 4 × 4 and 6 × 6 light trucks*)
Link Road, West Wilts Trading Estate, Westbury, Wiltshire BA13 4JB

RTV Ltd. (*RTV 4 × 4 – Ford-based light truck*)
PO Box 6, Sandford Avenue, Church Stretton, Shropshire SY6 7ZZ

South East Towing (*RAGE ROVER – Range Rover-based kit car*)
1 Rowhill Cottages, Puddledock Lane, Wilmington, Kent DA2 7QF

Supacat Ltd. (*Volkswagen-powered 6 × 6 all terrain vehicle*)
The Airport, Dunkeswell, Honiton, Devon

Wessex (UK) Plc. (*Bog Cogs – detachable traction aids*)
Unit 4, Porsham Close, Belliver Ind Est, Roborough, Plymouth, Devon

Winch & Winching Equipment Suppliers

Autosteer Controls – The Winch Wharehouse
Grangefield Ind Est, Richerdshaw Road, Pudsey, Leeds, Yorkshire LS28 6QW

Barmac International Ltd.
PO Box 28-083, Remurra, Auckland, New Zealand

Birmingham Rope & Tackle
Fawdry Street, Birmingham, West Midlands B9 4BG

Bushey Hall Transport Equipment
Bushey Hall Drive, Bushey, Watford, Hertfordshire WD2 2EP

FW Winches Ltd.
Abbey Rise, Whitchurch Road, Tavistock, Devon PL19 9DR

Goodwinch
East Foldhay, Zeal Monachorum, Crediton, Devon EX17 6OR

Ryders International
Knowsley Road, Bootle, Liverpool, Merseyside

Sepson AB
S-780 50 Vansbro, Sweden

Skidmore 4WD Ltd.
60 Sandwell Street, Walsall, West Midlands WS1 3EB

Superwinch – ICM 4 × 4 Equipment
Longridge, Preston, Lancashire

The Pinzgauer Explorer motor home (left) is built on the chassis of the 'ordinary' 6 × 6 Adventurer (right). For long-range off-road adventure holidays these vehicles offer unrivalled mobility and comfort.

FOUR WHEEL DRIVING